THE VULNERABLE WITNESSES (SCOTLAND) ACT 2004

T0386696

THE VULNERABLE WITNESSES (SCOTLAND) ACT 2004

Laura Sharp

Lecturer in Law and Course Leader for Diploma in Legal Practice, Robert Gordon University, Aberdeen

Margaret Ross

Head of Law, University of Aberdeen

DUNDEE UNIVERSITY PRESS
2008

First published in Great Britain in 2008 by
Dundee University Press
University of Dundee
Dundee DD1 4HN

www.dup.dundee.ac.uk

ISBN 978-1-84586-045-5

No natural forests were destroyed to make this product;
only farmed timber was used and replanted.

British Library Cataloguing-in-Publication Data
A catalogue record for this book is available on request from the British Library

Typeset by Pilmuir Graphics, Langholm
Printed and bound by Bell & Bain Ltd, Glasgow

CONTENTS

TABLE OF CASES

TABLE OF STATUTES

Page

TABLE OF STATUTORY INSTRUMENTS

Page

INTRODUCTION

An Act of the Scottish Parliament to make provision for the use of special measures for the purpose of taking the evidence of children and other vulnerable witnesses in criminal or civil proceedings; to provide for evidential presumptions in criminal proceedings where certain reports of identification procedures are lodged as productions; to make provision about the admissibility of expert psychological or psychiatric evidence as to subsequent behaviour of the complainer in criminal proceedings in respect of certain offences; to prohibit persons charged with certain offences from conducting their own defence at the trial and any victim statement proof where a child witness under the age of 12 is to give evidence at the trial; to enable the court to prohibit persons from conducting their own defence at the trial and any victim statement proof in other criminal proceedings in which a vulnerable witness is to give evidence; to prohibit persons charged with certain offences from seeking to precognosce personally a child under the age of 12; to make provision about the admissibility of certain evidence bearing on the character, conduct or condition of witnesses in proceedings before a sheriff relating to the establishment of grounds of referral to children's hearings; to abolish the competence test for witnesses in criminal and civil proceedings; and for connected purposes.

The Vulnerable Witnesses (Scotland) Act 2004 is the only statute thus far to be devoted to making provision to assist children and vulnerable adult witnesses to give evidence. Formerly, any such statutory measures had been contained in general criminal justice or miscellaneous provisions legislation. The Act brings about four principal changes.

First, "vulnerable witness" is now defined so as to include a much wider range of adult witnesses than previously and, for the first time, witnesses who have suffered or who fear intimidation may apply for the use of special measures. The Act also applies to the accused where he or she gives evidence and meets the criteria of vulnerability under the Act. Second, child witnesses now have an automatic entitlement to the use of one or more special measures, unless they wish to give evidence without them and the court believes that it is appropriate for them to do so. There is no need to establish that the quality of the witness's testimony would be adversely affected or that the child would suffer any distress in giving evidence in the traditional manner. Third, the 2004 Act differs from previous primary legislation in that, for the first time, it permits the court to authorise the use of special measures by vulnerable witnesses in civil cases including fatal accident inquiries and in court proceedings arising out of children's hearings. Finally, the Act abolishes the pre-testimony competence test for witnesses in criminal and civil proceedings. The Act also contains a number of incidental amendments to the rules of criminal evidence and procedure. Earlier provisions pertaining to vulnerable witnesses had applied initially to child witnesses and latterly to a limited range of adult witnesses in criminal proceedings only. There was limited provision for children to give evidence by live video link in care proceedings under the Act of Sederunt (Child Care and Maintenance Rules) 1997 (SI 1997/291), r 3.22. The pre-2004 Act provisions on the evidence of vulnerable witnesses in criminal cases were to be found in the Criminal Procedure (Scotland) Act 1995, s 271, as last amended with effect from 1 August 1997 by the Crime and Punishment (Scotland) Act 1997, s 29.

In civil cases the first provisions in primary legislation to assist child and adult vulnerable witnesses appear in the 2004 Act but there was express provision for video-link evidence of children in care proceedings from 1997. The scope to admit hearsay evidence in civil cases from 1988 under the Civil Evidence (Scotland) Act 1988, s 2 did not for some years lead to admission of statements in place of the evidence of children or vulnerable witnesses, because of the narrow interpretation of s 2 taken in *L v L* 1996 SLT 767, in which the hearsay evidence was said to be admissible only if the competence of the witness could be established in court. This reasoning held until disapproved in *T v T* 2000 SLT 1442.

Until 1991 in the case of children (those under the age of 16), and 1997 in that of adult vulnerable witnesses, all witnesses cited to give evidence in criminal proceedings were, with very few exceptions, subject to the same procedural rules. In criminal cases, the court had the power at common law to make the court as non-threatening an environment for a child witness as the preservation of the accused's right to a fair trial permitted. Such steps included the removal of formal court dress and the judge, witness, prosecutor and defence counsel or solicitor sitting together at a table in the well of the court rather than having the child testify from the witness box. However, such steps were not always viewed favourably by the Bench and research conducted between 1986 and 1989 revealed an inconsistent approach to their use (R Flin, R Bull, J Boon and A Knox, "Children in the Witness Box" in H Dent and R Flin (eds), *Children as Witnesses* 1992). The steps were re-emphasised in the Memorandum on Child Witnesses issued by the Lord Justice-General in 1990. The Criminal Procedure (Scotland) Act 1975, ss 166 and 362 did permit the court, while a child gave evidence "in any proceedings in relation to an offence against or any conduct contrary to morality", to exclude from the courtroom all those not directly connected with the conduct of the case, other than *bona fide* members of the press. Offences of violence or dishonesty or a road traffic accident were unlikely to have come within the ambit of those sections and yet giving evidence in such cases could have proved to have been a traumatic and distressing experience. No procedural concessions were made for adult witnesses with learning difficulties, those suffering from mental disorder or intimidated witnesses.

No single event brought about statutory reform of the law on the evidence of children. As recently as the mid-1980s, there was still doubt, even among some legal professionals, as to the extent of the adverse effect, if any, that giving evidence had on children. Calls for reform were met with some resistance from the legal establishment. The main grounds of opposition to reform were founded in a belief that the best evidence is testimony given by a witness in person in court in the presence of the accused, even if the quality and coherence of that evidence are adversely affected by the stress of appearing in court. In addition, no official records were kept of how many children were cited as witnesses or how many went on to give evidence at a trial diet, and so it was almost impossible to ascertain whether there was a need for reform.

The first empirical research to be carried out in the United Kingdom into the effect giving evidence in criminal cases had on child witnesses was funded by the Scottish Office and took place in Aberdeen and Glasgow between 1986 and 1989. The researchers noted that while the majority of children who testified were able to give evidence reasonably well, a high proportion of the 111 children they observed were anxious, unhappy or even tearful while they did so. The study questioned whether the rules of criminal evidence and procedure at that time enabled evidence of the best quality to be obtained from child witnesses, and whether alternative methods of taking evidence from them could be found which would alleviate their stress and anxiety without jeopardising the accused's right to a fair trial. Subsequent studies revealed that the issues which witnesses themselves found most distressing were: the need to confront the accused in open court; and being subjected to prolonged and potentially hostile cross-examination by the accused in person or his or her legal representatives. Both of these factors could cause the child to break down and be unable to continue, thus causing the case to fail.

The first statutory provisions to permit a child under the age of 14 to give evidence by means of a closed-circuit live television link in some, but not all, criminal cases were introduced in England and Wales in the Criminal Justice Act 1988, s 32. No comparable measures were introduced in Scotland at that time. The process which was to lead to the introduction of the first special measures in Scotland began with the preparation by the Scottish Law Commission of a Discussion Paper on *The Evidence of Children and other Potentially Vulnerable Witnesses* (Scot Law Com No 75, 1988). The Commission examined the existing law and practice for the giving of evidence by children and other potentially vulnerable witnesses in criminal proceedings and the difficulties which were believed to arise in cases in which children gave evidence. It investigated the techniques in use in other jurisdictions to assist child witnesses and considered what reforms it might be appropriate to introduce into the Scottish system while neither jeopardising the accused's right to a fair trial (protected by Art 6 of the European Convention on Human Rights) nor encroaching on the prohibition against the admissibility of hearsay evidence, nor removing the requirement for corroboration. Children were not considered to be vulnerable by reason of their age and the Discussion Paper proceeded on the assumption that even if change was indicated, in many cases children would continue to testify in court in the conventional manner.

Following a period of consultation, in 1990 the Scottish Law Commission issued its *Report on the Evidence of Children and Other Potentially Vulnerable Witnesses* (Scot Law Com No 125, 1990). The Report made a number of recommendations some of which, principally those permitting the court on cause shown to authorise child witnesses to give their evidence by means of the live television link, on commission or while screened from the accused's sight, formed the basis for legislative reforms between 1990 and 1993. Other recommendations were not implemented until much later. The extension of special measures to adult vulnerable witnesses, even to a limited extent, was not introduced until 1997 and others, such as the application of the provisions to civil cases and court proceedings arising out of children's hearings, are only now included in the 2004 Act.

In addition to the 1990 Report, the origins of the 2004 Act can also be seen in the results of two consultation exercises: *Towards a Just Conclusion* (Scottish Office, 1998–2000) and *Vital Voices: Helping Vulnerable Witnesses to Give Evidence* (Scottish Executive, 2002–03). The Act improves upon existing rules of criminal procedure on vulnerable witnesses which were enacted in various forms between 1990 and 1997 and makes some further changes such as the abolition of the competence test for witnesses in civil and criminal proceedings that apply to all witnesses (although they are likely to be of most relevance to child witnesses and adults with learning difficulties or suffering from a mental disorder).

The 2004 Act is divided into three parts and has 24 substantive sections: Pt 1 (ss 1–10) deals with criminal proceedings; Pt 2 (ss 11–23) with civil proceedings; and Pt 3 (ss 24 and 25) with the abolition of the competence test for witnesses in civil and criminal cases, commencement and the short title. Sections 1–10 amend existing legislation, principally the Criminal Procedure (Scotland) Act 1995 but also the Criminal Justice (Scotland) Act 2003. The 2004 Act will be the primary authority for topics dealt with in Pts 2 and 3.

The Vulnerable Witnesses (Scotland) Bill was presented to the Scottish Parliament on 23 June 2003. It was scrutinised by the Justice 2 Committee, chaired by Annabel Goldie MSP, between September and December 2003. At Stage 1 of the Bill the Committee heard evidence and written submissions from witnesses representing the criminal justice agencies and other interested parties. Although the drafting of the Bill was criticised by some members of the committee as being difficult to follow, there was very little disagreement in principle over the need to improve the lot of vulnerable witnesses, in particular in criminal proceedings. Repeated reference was made during the passage of the Bill to the need not only for legislative change but for a change in culture and attitude to the way in which all witnesses, and vulnerable witnesses in particular, were treated. The Bill was considered by the Parliament in November 2003 and again on 4 March 2004 when it was passed. It received the Royal Assent on 14 April 2004. The Act as passed is similar to the Bill in most essentials, although substantial amendments were required to the provisions on child witnesses to ensure that they would fulfil the policy intentions of the Scottish Executive. The Policy Memorandum accompanying the Bill had spoken in terms of child witnesses having a "right" to use a special measure. However, as drafted, the Bill appeared to grant only the same discretionary entitlement afforded to adult witnesses. Witnesses to the Justice 2 Committee were critical of this aspect of the Bill, noting that there was no practical difference between those terms of the Bill and the existing law, and that it gave children no protection from arbitrary decisions not to grant the special measures requested. As a result, a group of amendments intended to offer a simplified procedure for dealing with the majority of child witness cases was successfully moved by Karen Whitefield MSP. These had the effect of ensuring that child witnesses do have an automatic entitlement to use one or more of a group of what are known as "standard special measures": the live television link or the use of a screen, with or without the presence of a supporter.

Implementation of the Act commenced on 1 April 2005, with the enactment of some provisions, such as the abolition of the competence test in all cases and the introduction of special measures in solemn criminal cases involving child witnesses reported to the procurator fiscal on or after 1 April 2005, and court proceedings arising out of children's hearings. The Act came into force on 1 April 2006 in respect of adult vulnerable witnesses in solemn cases reported to the procurator fiscal on or after 1 April 2006. It was introduced for child witnesses in summary criminal cases in the sheriff court on 1 April 2007 and in respect of all vulnerable witnesses in all non-criminal cases with effect from 1 November 2007. The final phase of implementation for adult vulnerable witnesses in summary criminal cases took place in April 2008. The provisions do not as yet apply to criminal proceedings in the district court, but s 10 of the 2004 Act inserts a new s 288G into the 1995 Act which grants the power to the Scottish Ministers to order by statutory instrument that the Act should apply to proceedings there.

The Scottish Government has produced a wide range of explanatory information in booklet and CD-ROM formats for children, young persons and adults on being a witness, on going to court in criminal and civil cases and proceedings arising out of children's hearings, of the measures available and the circumstances in which they can be used. It has also provided guidance for parents of child witnesses and carers of adults with learning disabilities on what can be expected from the court process. Booklets are available in age-appropriate language. Translations of these materials are available in Arabic, Bengali, Cantonese, Gaelic, Hindi, Polish, Punjabi and Urdu and can be accessed at http://www.scotland.gov. uk/Topics/. A link to the Witnesses in Scotland website (http://www. witnessesinscotland.com) is also provided from the same site.

1 DEFINITIONS OF "VULNERABLE WITNESS" IN CIVIL AND CRIMINAL CASES AND THE SPECIAL MEASURES

VULNERABLE WITNESS (1995 ACT, S 271; 2004 ACT, S 1)

The definition of "vulnerable witness" in criminal proceedings can be found in the 2004 Act, s 1 which substitutes ss 271–271M for the existing s 271 of the Criminal Procedure (Scotland) Act 1995 (the "1995 Act"). In civil proceedings the definition is contained in s 11 of the 2004 Act. The definition is in identical terms for both types of proceedings.

1 Evidence of children and other vulnerable witnesses: special measures

(1) For section 271 (evidence of vulnerable persons: special provision) of the Criminal Procedure (Scotland) Act 1995 (c. 46) (referred to in this Part as "the 1995 Act") there is substituted—

"Special measures for child witnesses and other vulnerable witnesses

271 Vulnerable witnesses: main definitions

(1) For the purposes of this Act, a person who is giving or is to give evidence at, or for the purposes of, a trial is a vulnerable witness if—
   (a) the person is under the age of 16 on the date of commencement of the proceedings in which the trial is being or to be held (such a vulnerable witness being referred to in this Act as a "child witness"), or
   (b) where the person is not a child witness, there is a significant risk that the quality of the evidence to be given by the person will be diminished by reason of—
       (i) mental disorder (within the meaning of section 328 of the Mental Health (Care and Treatment) (Scotland) Act 2003 (asp 13)), or
       (ii) fear or distress in connection with giving evidence at the trial.

(2) In determining whether a person is a vulnerable witness by virtue of subsection (1)(b) above, the court shall take into account—

    (a) the nature and circumstances of the alleged offence to which the proceedings relate,

    (b) the nature of the evidence which the person is likely to give,

    (c) the relationship (if any) between the person and the accused,

    (d) the person's age and maturity,

    (e) any behaviour towards the person on the part of—

        (i) the accused,

        (ii) members of the family or associates of the accused,

        (iii) any other person who is likely to be an accused or a witness in the proceedings, and

    (f) such other matters, including—

        (i) the social and cultural background and ethnic origins of the person,

        (ii) the person's sexual orientation,

        (iii) the domestic and employment circumstances of the person,

        (iv) any religious beliefs or political opinions of the person, and

        (v) any physical disability or other physical impairment which the person has,

    as appear to the court to be relevant.

(3) For the purposes of subsection (1)(a) above and section 271B(1)(b) below, proceedings shall be taken to have commenced when the indictment or, as the case may be, complaint is served on the accused.

(4) In subsection (1)(b) above, the reference to the quality of evidence is to its quality in terms of completeness, coherence and accuracy.

(5) In this section and sections 271A to 271M of this Act—

    "court" means the High Court or the sheriff court,

    "trial" means a trial under solemn procedure in any court or under summary procedure in the sheriff court.

(6) In sections 271A to 271M of this Act, "special measure" means any of the special measures set out in, or prescribed under, section 271H below.

11 Interpretation of this Part

(1) For the purposes of this Part of this Act, a person who is giving or is to give evidence in or for the purposes of any civil proceedings is a vulnerable witness if—

    (a) the person is under the age of 16 on the date of commencement of the proceedings (such a vulnerable witness being referred to in this Part as a "child witness"), or

    (b) where the person is not a child witness, there is a significant risk that the quality of the evidence to be given by the person will be diminished by reason of—

        (i) mental disorder (within the meaning of section 328 of the Mental Health (Care and Treatment) (Scotland) Act 2003 (asp 13)), or

        (ii) fear or distress in connection with giving evidence in the proceedings.

(2) In considering whether a person is a vulnerable witness by virtue of subsection (1)(b) above, the court must take into account—

    (a) the nature and circumstances of the alleged matter to which the proceedings relate,

    (b) the nature of the evidence which the person is likely to give,

    (c) the relationship (if any) between the person and any party to the proceedings,

    (d) the person's age and maturity,

    (e) any behaviour towards the person on the part of—

        (i) any party to the proceedings,

        (ii) members of the family or associates of any such party,

        (iii) any other person who is likely to be a party to the proceedings or a witness in the proceedings, and

    (f) such other matters, including—

        (i) the social and cultural background and ethnic origins of the person,

        (ii) the person's sexual orientation,

        (iii) the domestic and employment circumstances of the person,

        (iv) any religious beliefs or political opinions of the person, and

        (v) any physical disability or other physical impairment which the person has,

    as appear to the court to be relevant.

(3) For the purposes of subsection (1)(a) above, proceedings are taken to have commenced when the petition, summons, initial writ or other document initiating the proceedings is served, and, where the document is served on more than one person, the proceedings shall be taken to have commenced when the document is served on the first person on whom it is served.

(4) In subsection (1)(b), the reference to the quality of evidence is to its quality in terms of completeness, coherence and accuracy.

(5) In this Part—

    "child witness notice" has the meaning given in section 12(2),

"civil proceedings" includes, in addition to such proceedings in any of the ordinary courts of law, any proceedings to which section 91 (procedural rules in relation to certain applications etc.) of the Children (Scotland) Act 1995 (c. 36) applies,
"court" is to be construed in accordance with the meaning of "civil proceedings",
"special measure" means any of the special measures set out in, or prescribed under, section 18,
"vulnerable witness application" has the meaning given in section 12(6)(a).

Child witnesses

A person who is giving or is to give evidence under solemn procedure in the High Court or the sheriff court or under summary procedure in the sheriff court as a witness for the prosecution or for the defence, or in any civil proceedings, is a vulnerable witness if he or she is under the age of 16 on the date of commencement of the proceedings (1995 Act, s 271(1)(a) and 2004 Act, s 11(1)(a)). Proceedings are held to have commenced when the indictment or complaint is served on the accused (1995 Act, s 271(3)) or when the document initiating proceedings is served (2004 Act, s 11(3)). Should the trial or proof be delayed, the witness will still be entitled to use the special measures even though he or she has reached the age of 16 by the time it begins. Previously, children who had turned 16 by the time the trial took place were not eligible for the use of statutory special measures but might have been able to move the court to use its common law powers to permit a supporter to be present with them while they gave their evidence, or to give evidence from behind a screen. In cases where the child turns 16 between the date of the conduct which is the subject of the proceedings and the service of the indictment, complaint or other initiating document, then there is a possibility that he or she may satisfy the criteria of "adult vulnerable witness" defined in the 1995 Act, s 271(1)(b)(i) and (ii) and the 2004 Act, s 11(1)(b), or persuade the court to exercise its common law powers in criminal cases (described below) which are expressly preserved by the 1995 Act, s 271G.

Adult vulnerable witnesses

Previously, under the Criminal Procedure (Scotland) Act 1995, s 271(12)(b) "vulnerable person" meant a person of 16 years of age or over who was subject to an order made by a court in any part of the United Kingdom under its mental health legislation that he or she was suffering from a mental disorder; or who was subject to a transfer direction under that legislation; or who otherwise appeared to the court to suffer from significant impairment of intelligence and social functioning. This definition was very restrictive and was criticised for excluding many adult witnesses who might have benefited from some assistance in giving evidence. However, it was possible for adult witnesses who did not meet the criteria of s 271(12)(b) to seek the authorisation of the court for its common law powers to allow them to give evidence while screened from the sight of the accused or while accompanied by a support person. In *Hampson and Others* v *HM Advocate* 2003 SCCR 13, the adult complainer in a rape trial, while suffering from a mental disorder, did not come within the terms of s 271(12)(b). The High Court upheld the decision of the court at a preliminary diet to permit her to give her evidence while protected by a screen, stating that the court had "the power and, indeed, the duty" at common law to regulate its proceedings and in particular in relation to the way in which witnesses are permitted to give their evidence. The court required to be satisfied that if the application was granted, the arrangements would not inevitably result in the accused having an unfair trial (*Smith* v *HM Advocate* 2000 SCCR 910). *McGinley* v *HM Advocate* 2001 SCCR 47 established that in appropriate cases adult witnesses could be permitted to have a support person in court with them while they gave their evidence.

Under the 2004 Act, where the witness is not a child, if there is "a significant risk that the quality of the evidence to be given by the person will be diminished" by reason of either mental disorder or fear or distress in connection with giving evidence at the trial, the person is also a vulnerable witness. "Quality" means its quality in terms of "completeness, coherence and accuracy". "Mental disorder" has the same meaning as in the Mental Health (Care and Treatment) (Scotland) Act 2003, s 328(1) in which it is defined as "any mental illness, personality disorder or learning disability however caused or manifested". A person is not mentally disordered by reason only of sexual orientation or deviancy, transsexualism, transvestism, dependence on drugs or alcohol, behaviour that causes or is likely to cause harassment or alarm or distress to any other person, or acting as no other prudent person would act (2003 Act, s 328(2)).

To assist the court in deciding whether a person is a vulnerable witness, the 1995 Act, s 271(2) and the 2004 Act, s 11(2) set out a list of factors which it is required to take into account. These include the nature and circumstances of the alleged offence or matter; the nature of the evidence which the person is going to give; the relationship between the witness and the accused or party; and the age and maturity of the witness. The court is also required to take account of any behaviour towards the witness on the part of: the accused or a party; members of his or her family or associates; or any other person who is likely to be an accused, a party or a witness in the case. This subsection grants the power to the court for the first time to offer statutory protection to witnesses who are or might be subject to intimidation. Previously, if concerns existed about the risk of intimidation of witnesses in criminal cases, then the witness had to depend on the court exercising its discretion at common law to permit the witness to give evidence anonymously from behind a screen where the personal safety of the witness was in issue. This measure was used in *HM Advocate* v *Smith and Others* 2000 SCCR 910, where the witnesses were undercover police officers.

The court must also take into account such other matters as appears to it to be relevant, such as the witness's ethnic origins and social and cultural background; sexual orientation; employment and domestic circumstances; religious beliefs or political opinions; and any physical disabilities or impairments he or she might have. This list is not intended to be exhaustive, but is an indication of what might have a bearing on whether a witness meets the criteria of s 271(1)(b) or s 11(1)(b). In each case the court will require to take into account the individual circumstances of the witness, the nature of the case and the evidence to be given.

It is anticipated that the scope of s 271(2) will greatly increase the number of adult witnesses in criminal proceedings who might qualify for the use of special measures under the 2004 Act compared with those who were eligible under the earlier provisions, and s 11(2) brings the option to civil courts expressly for the first time. Now in both criminal and civil proceedings there appears to be scope for witnesses to be classed as vulnerable at one stage in their lives but not another, or in one case but not in another, depending on the nature of any mental disorder or the type of case in which they are witnesses. For example, a woman who is a bystander witness to a theft from a supermarket would not ordinarily be classed as a vulnerable person, but if she were diagnosed as suffering from depression or some other mental disorder at the time of the trial, she might be. If the same woman were to be called to give evidence as the complainer in a historic sexual abuse case or in a case concerning residence of her children following domestic abuse, she might be held to be a vulnerable witness even though she was not suffering from any mental disorder. A mental disorder does not need to be so serious as to require that the witness is the subject of a court order under the mental health legislation in order for it to be taken into consideration by the court.

THE SPECIAL MEASURES (1995 ACT, S 271H; 2004 ACT, S 18)

271H *The special measures*

(1) The special measures which may be authorised to be used under section 271A, 271C or 271D of this Act for the purpose of taking the evidence of a vulnerable witness are—

(a) taking of evidence by a commissioner in accordance with section 271I of this Act,

(b) *use of a live television link in accordance with section 271J of this Act,*

(c) *use of a screen in accordance with section 271K of this Act,*

(d) *use of a supporter in accordance with section 271L of this Act,*

(e) *giving evidence in chief in the form of a prior statement in accordance with section 271M of this Act, and*

(f) *such other measures as the Scottish Ministers may, by order made by statutory instrument, prescribe.*

(2) *An order under subsection (1)(f) above shall not be made unless a draft of the statutory instrument containing the order has been laid before and approved by a resolution of the Scottish Parliament.*

(3) *Provision may be made by Act of Adjournal regulating, so far as not regulated by sections 271I to 271M of this Act, the use in any proceedings of any special measure authorised to be used by virtue of section 271A, 271C or 271D of this Act.*

18 The special measures

(1) *The special measures which may be authorised to be used by virtue of section 12 or 13 of this Act for the purpose of taking the evidence of a vulnerable witness are—*

(a) *taking of evidence by a commissioner in accordance with section 19,*

(b) *use of a live television link in accordance with section 20,*

(c) *use of screen in accordance with section 21,*

(d) *use of a supporter in accordance with section 22, and*

(e) *such other measures as the Scottish Ministers may, by order made by statutory instrument, prescribe.*

(2) *An order under subsection (1)(e) above is not to be made unless a draft of the statutory instrument containing the order has been laid before and approved by a resolution of the Scottish Parliament.*

The special measures are now set out in s 271H of the 1995 Act and s 18 of the 2004 Act. All the measures, other than the giving of evidence in chief in the form of a prior statement which has not been video recorded, are designed to ensure that the accused is able to see and hear the witness give evidence in chief. They do not interfere with the accused's right *inter alia* to examine and have examined witnesses against him, guaranteed in Art 6(3)(d) of the European Convention on Human Rights, in that they all enable the accused to see and hear the witness being cross-examined. Section 271H(1)(f) of the 1995 Act and s 18(1)(e) of the 2004 Act provide that the Scottish Ministers may by order prescribe additional special measures.

The taking of evidence by a commissioner (1995 Act, s 271I; 2004 Act, s 19)

271I Taking of evidence by a commissioner

(1) Where the special measure to be used is taking of evidence by a commissioner, the court shall appoint a commissioner to take the evidence of the vulnerable witness in respect of whom the special measure is to be used.

(2) Proceedings before a commissioner appointed under subsection (1) above shall be recorded by video recorder.

(3) An accused—
  (a) shall not, except by leave of the court on special cause shown, be present in the room where such proceedings are taking place, but
  (b) is entitled by such means as seem suitable to the court to watch and hear the proceedings.

(4) The recording of the proceedings made in pursuance of subsection (2) above shall be received in evidence without being sworn to by witnesses.

19 Taking of evidence by a commissioner

(1) Where the special measure to be used is taking of evidence by a commissioner, the court must appoint a commissioner to take the evidence of the vulnerable witness in respect of whom the special measure is to be used.

(2) Proceedings before a commissioner appointed under subsection (1) above must be recorded by video recorder.

(3) A party to the proceedings—
  (a) must not, except by leave of the court, be present in the room where such proceedings are taking place, but
  (b) is entitled by such means as seem suitable to the court to watch and hear the proceedings.

(4) The recording of the proceedings made in pursuance of subsection (2) above is to be received in evidence without being sworn to by witnesses.

The court may appoint a commissioner to take the evidence of a vulnerable witness in advance of the trial. The commissioner might be the judge in the case or a judge of the relevant court who must be able to rule on any questions of admissibility that may arise during the commission. Despite the wording of the sections which suggests that he examines the witness himself, the commissioner presides over proceedings but the witness is examined and cross-examined by the parties conducting the case, in accordance with the principles of the adversarial system. The witness will be asked to swear or promise to tell the truth before he or she is questioned. Ordinarily the accused is not permitted to be present in the room where proceedings are taking place, other than by the leave of the court on special cause shown, but is entitled to watch and hear proceedings while the evidence is taken, for example by means of a live television link. In civil proceedings a party must not, except by leave of the court, be present during the proceedings on commission. This appears to mean *any* party, including the party who has called the witness, but that party may more readily obtain leave and no party in civil proceedings is required to show the special cause that an accused must show. Indeed, it is possible that a party might also be the designated supporter for the witness in accordance with another special measure discussed below.

Proceedings on commission are video recorded and the recording is received in evidence at the trial or proof without being sworn to by the witness. The recording can then be used at a suitable stage in the trial or proof without the witness having to appear. It is anticipated that the commissioner and parties conducting the case will not wear formal court attire, in accordance with *High Court of Justiciary Practice Note, Child Witnesses: Discretionary Powers, No 2 of 2005* in criminal proceedings, and normal practice for taking evidence on commission in civil proceedings.

Although evidence on commission has been available in criminal cases as a statutory special measure since 1994 for children and 1997 for adult vulnerable witnesses, it is a measure which has seldom, if ever, been used. In contrast, taking evidence on commission has had a long history in civil cases at common law in any situation where a witness would have difficulty in attending court for the proof and the evidence is therefore at risk of being lost (although its use diminished to some extent after hearsay evidence became generally admissible in civil cases). Although the exact reasons for the low usage in criminal cases are unknown, it is the most technically complex and requires the greatest amount of forward planning of all the special measures. It also requires all parties to be fully prepared in advance of the commencement of the trial or proof itself, and to be able to gather in person in one place in order for the full testimony of the witness to be obtained and recorded. This may be the nearest suitably equipped court to the witness's home which may be some distance for the parties conducting the case to travel, but mobile equipment could even allow the witness (at least in civil cases) to give evidence from a domestic setting while those parties have contemporaneous access to the recording of that evidence in suitably equipped premises.

Despite the practical and technical complexities associated with the taking of evidence by a commissioner, it is likely to be used in particular in criminal trials of sexual or violent offences involving children under the age of 12 when proceedings commence. This is because, in terms of s 271B(3), the court must not make an order authorising the use of special measures in such cases that would have the effect of the child giving evidence in the same court building as the trial, unless either the child has expressed a wish and the court considers that it is appropriate for the child to be so present, or the taking of the evidence of the child witness without the child being present in the building would give risk to a significant risk of prejudice to the fairness of the trial or the interests of justice and the risk significantly outweighs any risk of prejudice to the interests of the child if the order is made. At present, the only special measures which enable s 271B(3) to be complied with are the taking of evidence by a commissioner or the use of a live television link from a remote location. The success of the measure depends on adequate provision being made across Scotland of suitably equipped facilities to make this measure a practicable choice.

Live television link (1995 Act, s 271J; 2004 Act, s 20)

271J Live television link

(1) Where the special measure to be used is a live television link, the court shall make such arrangements as seem to it appropriate for the vulnerable witness in respect of whom the special measure is to be used to give evidence from a place outside the court-room where the trial is to take place by means of a live television link between that place and the court-room.

(2) The place from which the vulnerable witness gives evidence by means of the link—
  (a) may be another part of the court building in which the court-room is located or any other suitable place outwith that building, and
  (b) shall be treated, for the purposes of the proceedings at the trial, as part of the court-room whilst the witness is giving evidence.

(3) Any proceedings conducted by means of a live television link by virtue of this section shall be treated as taking place in the presence of the accused.

(4) Where—
  (a) the live television link is to be used in proceedings in a sheriff court, but
  (b) that court lacks accommodation or equipment necessary for the purpose of receiving such a link,
  the sheriff may by order transfer the proceedings to any other sheriff court in the same sheriffdom which has such accommodation or equipment available.

(5) *An order may be made under subsection (4) above—*

    (a) *at any stage in the proceedings (whether before or after the commencement of the trial), or*

    (b) *in relation to any part of the proceedings.*

20 Live television link

(1) *Where the special measure to be used is a live television link, the court must make such arrangements as seem to it appropriate for the vulnerable witness in respect of whom the special measure is to be used to give evidence by means of such a link.*

(2) *Where—*

    (a) *the live television link is to be used in proceedings in a sheriff court, but*

    (b) *that court lacks accommodation or equipment necessary for the purpose of receiving such a link,*

    the sheriff may by order transfer the proceedings to any sheriff court in the same sheriffdom which has such accommodation or equipment available.

(3) *An order may be made under subsection (2) above—*

    (a) *at any stage in the proceedings (whether before or after the commencement of the proof or other hearing at which the vulnerable witness is to give evidence), or*

    (b) *in relation to a part of the proceedings.*

This was the first statutory special measure to be introduced for criminal proceedings in Scotland: it emerged in 1991. The 2004 Act makes provision for the vulnerable witness to give evidence by means of a live television link either from a witness room in the court building or in any other suitable place outwith the building. This may be a room in an appropriate non-court building or another court building. The TV monitors, cameras and microphones used in the live television link system introduced in Scotland are controlled by the judge or sheriff who may intervene at any time to turn off the equipment if, for example, an objection as to the nature of the questioning is made. The witness sits in the witness room in front of a television screen, cameras and a microphone and will usually see and hear only the person in the courtroom who is speaking to him at any particular time. The accused can see and hear the witness give evidence by way of a television monitor situated in or near the dock but the witness does not see the accused. A separate monitor is provided for the jury. Those conducting the case have television monitors, cameras and microphones which enable them to see and hear the witness and the witness to see and hear them as they speak. Their monitors show, by a split-screen method, the face of the witness and the person speaking to him. The judge or sheriff has a full view of the room where the witness is situated and any support person with him and also sees the same images as those conducting the case.

Not all courts in Scotland are or will be equipped with the live television link. In 2003, nine of Scotland's 52 courthouses had live television link equipment. When the Bill was introduced, the Scottish Executive made financial provision for the equipping of 10 more courts and for the setting up of remote witness suites to enable witnesses, in particular those under the age of 12, to give evidence to the court via a live television link from outwith the court building. A list of all the courtroom technology facilities currently available in courts in Scotland can be viewed at: http://www.scotcourts.gov.uk/courtusers/witnesses/vulnerablewitness.asp.

Access to all live television links is managed by the Scottish Court Service Electronic Service Delivery Unit (ESDU). Details of all applications for live television link must be intimated to ESDU at as early a stage in proceedings as possible before the child witness notice or vulnerable witness application is lodged with the court. The form for notifying ESDU and the protocol for managing live television links and monitoring the demand for the measure devised by the Vulnerable Witness Implementation and Steering Group can be viewed at and downloaded from: http://www.scotcourts.gov.uk/courtusers/witnesses/vulnerablewitness.asp.

In the event that the live television link is to be used in a sheriff court case but the court lacks the necessary accommodation or equipment, the sheriff may order the transfer of proceedings to a suitably equipped sheriff court elsewhere in the same sheriffdom.

Screens (1995 Act, s 271K; 2004 Act, s 21)

271K Screens

(1) *Where the special measure to be used is a screen, the screen shall be used to conceal the accused from the sight of the vulnerable witness in respect of whom the special measure is to be used.*

(2) *However, the court shall make arrangements to ensure that the accused is able to watch and hear the vulnerable witness giving evidence.*

(3) *Subsections (4) and (5) of section 271J of this Act apply for the purpose of the use of a screen under this section as they apply for the purpose of the use of a live television link under that section but as if—*
   (a) *references to the live television link were references to the screen, and*
   (b) *the reference to receiving such a link were a reference to the use of a screen.*

21 Screens

(1) Where the special measure to be used is a screen, the screen must be used to conceal the parties to the proceedings from the sight of the vulnerable witness in respect of whom the special measure is to be used.

(2) However, the court must make arrangements to ensure that the parties are able to watch and hear the vulnerable witness giving evidence.

(3) Subsections (2) and (3) of section 20 apply for the purposes of use of a screen under this section as they apply for the purposes of use of a live television link under that section but as if—
   (a) references to the live television link were references to the screen, and
   (b) the reference to receiving such a link were a reference to the use of a screen.

Where the witness is to give evidence in the courtroom, the screen is used to conceal the accused from the sight of the witness. The screen is positioned so that the witness cannot see the accused or the party but the parties conducting the trial or proof, the jury in solemn criminal cases and any members of the public and press present can see the accused at all times and the witness as he or she gives evidence. The accused or party can see the witness on a television monitor via a small camera placed in the witness box. This measure has been available in criminal cases under statute since 1994. Approval for the use of screens in criminal cases in England and Wales had been given by the Court of Appeal in 1989 in *R* v *X*, *R* v *Y and R* v Z (1990) 1991 Cr App R 36 and so their use had come to be accepted by the criminal courts in Scotland before they became available under statute. Different types of screens can be used. Some are moveable partitions to screen off the witness box from the rest of the courtroom and others are curtains designed to fit around the witness box. As with the live television link, if the court lacks the necessary equipment or accommodation, the sheriff may order the transfer of a case to a suitably equipped court elsewhere in the same sheriffdom.

Supporters (1995 Act, s 271L; 2004 Act, s 22)

271L Supporters

(1) Where the special measure to be used is a supporter, another person ("the supporter") nominated by or on behalf of the vulnerable witness in respect of whom the special measure is to be used may be present alongside the witness to support the witness while the witness is giving evidence.

(2) *Where the person nominated as the supporter is to give evidence at the trial, that person may not act as the supporter at any time before giving evidence.*

(3) *The supporter shall not prompt or otherwise seek to influence the witness in the course of giving evidence.*

22 Supporters

(1) *Where the special measure to be used is a supporter, another person ("the supporter") nominated by or on behalf of the vulnerable witness in respect of whom the special measure is to be used may be present alongside the witness for the purpose of providing support whilst the witness is giving evidence.*

(2) *Where the person nominated as the supporter is to give evidence in the proceedings, that person may not act as the supporter at any time before giving evidence.*

(3) *The supporter must not prompt or otherwise seek to influence the vulnerable witness in the course of giving evidence.*

This is a new statutory measure under the 2004 Act, but the use of a supporter has been permitted at the discretion of the court for some time. The Lord Justice-General's Memorandum on Child Witnesses of 26 July 1990 encouraged judges to permit a child witness to be accompanied by a support person while giving evidence and in *McGinley* v *HM Advocate* 2001 SCCR 47 the presence of a support person for an adult witness was considered appropriate in the circumstances. Under the 2004 Act, a person nominated by or on behalf of the vulnerable witness is permitted to be present alongside the witness to support him or her while the witness gives evidence in the courtroom or the room where the witness is to give evidence by live television link. The supporter also keeps the witness company in the witness room prior to his giving evidence and during any adjournments. Supporters provide emotional and social support. If the nominated support person is also a witness in the case, then he or she may not fulfil the role of supporter until his or her testimony is concluded. The supporter must not prompt or otherwise seek to influence the witness in the course of giving evidence. The use of a supporter is not classed as a standard special measure for criminal proceedings unless it is used in combination with the live television link or a screen. However, it can be sought as a measure by itself in criminal or civil proceedings, provided the party citing the witness can satisfy the court that the use of a supporter is the most appropriate measure in the circumstances of the witness and the case.

Giving evidence in chief in the form of a prior statement (1995 Act, s 271M: criminal cases only)

271M Giving evidence in chief in the form of a prior statement

(1) *This section applies where the special measure to be used in respect of a vulnerable witness is giving evidence in chief in the form of a prior statement.*

(2) *A statement made by the vulnerable witness which is lodged in evidence for the purposes of this section by or on behalf of the party citing the vulnerable witness shall, subject to subsection (3) below, be admissible as the witness's evidence in chief, or as part of the witness's evidence in chief, without the witness being required to adopt or otherwise speak to the statement in giving evidence in court.*

(3) *Section 260 of this Act shall apply to a statement lodged for the purposes of this section as it applies to a prior statement referred to in that section but as if—*
   (a) *references to a prior statement were references to the statement lodged for the purposes of this section,*
   (b) *in subsection (1), the words "where a witness gives evidence in criminal proceedings" were omitted, and*
   (c) *in subsection (2), paragraph (b) were omitted.*

(4) *This section does not affect the admissibility of any statement made by any person which is admissible otherwise than by virtue of this section.*

(5) *In this section, "statement" has the meaning given in section 262(1) of this Act.".*

(2) *In section 307(1) (interpretation) of the 1995 Act, there is inserted at the appropriate place in alphabetical order the following definitions—*
   ""child witness" shall be construed in accordance with section 271(1)(a) of this Act;",
   ""vulnerable witness" shall be construed in accordance with section 271(1) of this Act;".

This section permits a statement made by the vulnerable witness which is lodged in evidence to be admitted as the witness's evidence in chief, or part thereof, in criminal proceedings only. Such a measure is unnecessary in civil cases, where hearsay evidence is admissible generally under the Civil Evidence (Scotland) Act 1988, s 2. For criminal cases this is an entirely new special measure which owes much to the terms of s 260 of the 1995 Act (on admissibility of prior statements of witnesses). The prior statement must be contained in a document. This includes: a document in writing; any map, plan, graph or drawing; photograph; disc, tape or soundtrack; film, negative, tape, disc or other device for recording sound or visual images. However, unlike s 260, the witness is not required to adopt or otherwise speak to the statement in giving evidence in court. Although the Act is silent on the means of recording of the statement, it will require to be reliably recorded in some medium. Video recording appears to be the most appropriate method, as it would permit a fuller assessment of the witness's reliability and credibility and the nature of the line of questioning than a statement noted in a police notebook, for example. The practical value of this measure remains to be seen because, unless the statement has been agreed by all parties, the witness is still required to be available for cross-examination, either in court or by means of the live television link. If the statement cannot be agreed, the witness will, most likely, be called and be required to swear or promise to tell the truth before the prior statement is introduced as evidence. The Act does not specify whether the witness requires to be present in the court or the live television link room while the statement is being read or played to the court. If so, and the evidence is of a traumatic nature, the witness might be distressed at having to hear or see again what they said in the prior statement. On the other hand, if the witness does not hear the evidence in chief, he or she may find it difficult to answer questions on a statement made some time before and the precise detail of which might be forgotten. It might also be difficult for a young child or an adult with learning difficulties to understand the concept of being questioned on the content of a statement rather than what they recall of the incident or conduct complained of at the time they are cross-examined. The use of a prior statement as evidence in chief will also in many cases require the use of some other measure or measures, such as the live television link or a screen, to assist the vulnerable witness to answer questions in cross- and re–examination. The use of a combination of special measures may prove to be unnecessarily complicated and ultimately counterproductive. While what is the most appropriate special measure will vary from case to case, in many circumstances it might be more practicable and less confusing for the witness to use the live television link or screen for the whole of his or her testimony.

Standard special measures (1995 Act, s 271A(5)(a)(i) and (14); 2004 Act, s 12(1)(a) and (3))

271A Child witnesses

(5) The court shall, not later than 7 days after a child witness notice has been lodged, consider the notice in the absence of the parties and, subject to section 271B(3) of this Act—

(a) in the case of a notice under subsection (2)(a) above—

    (i) if a standard special measure is specified in the notice, make an order authorising the use of that measure for the purpose of taking the child witness's evidence, and

    (ii) if any other special measure is specified in the notice and the court is satisfied on the basis of the notice that it is appropriate to do so, make an order authorising the use of the special measure (in addition to any authorised by virtue of an order under sub-paragraph (i) above) for the purpose of taking the child witness's evidence,

(b) in the case of a notice under subsection (2)(b) above, if—

    (i) the summary of views accompanying the notice under subsection (3)(a) above indicates that the child witness has expressed a wish to give evidence without the benefit of any special measure, and

    (ii) the court is satisfied on the basis of the notice that it is appropriate to do so,

make an order authorising the giving of evidence by the child witness without the benefit of any special measure, or

(c) if—

    (i) paragraph (a)(ii) or (b) above would apply but for the fact that the court is not satisfied as mentioned in that paragraph, or

    (ii) in the case of a notice under subsection (2)(b), the summary of views accompanying the notice under subsection (3)(a) above indicates that the child witness has not expressed a wish to give evidence without the benefit of any special measure,

make an order under subsection (5A) below . . .

(14) In this section, references to a standard special measure are to any of the following special measures—

(a) the use of a live television link in accordance with section 271J of this Act where the place from which the child witness is to give evidence by means of the link is another part of the court building in which the court-room is located,

(b) the use of a screen in accordance with section 271K of this Act, and

(c) the use of a supporter in accordance with section 271L of this Act in conjunction with either of the special measures referred to in paragraphs (a) and (b) above.

12 Orders authorising the use of special measures for vulnerable witnesses

(1) Where a child witness is to give evidence in or for the purposes of any civil proceedings, the court must, before the proof or other hearing at which the child is to give evidence, make an order—

    (a) authorising the use of such special measure or measures as the court considers to be the most appropriate for the purpose of taking the child witness's evidence, or . . .

(3) If a child witness notice specifies any of the following special measures, namely—

    (a) the use of a live television link in accordance with section 20 where the place from which the child witness is to give evidence by means of the link is another part of the court building in which the court-room is located,

    (b) the use of a screen in accordance with section 21, or

    (c) the use of a supporter in accordance with section 22 in conjunction with either of the special measures referred to in paragraphs (a) and (b) above,

that special measure is, for the purposes of subsection (1)(a) above, to be taken to be the most appropriate for the purposes of taking the child witness's evidence.

For the purpose of child witness cases only, the use of the live television link, the use of a screen and the use of a supporter in combination with either the live television link or a screen are defined as standard special measures in criminal proceedings (1995 Act, s 271A(14)). In both civil and criminal cases, where authorisation for the use of those special measures is sought by the party citing the witness, the court must grant that authorisation (1995 Act, s 271A(5)(a)(i); and 2004 Act, s 12(1)(a) and (3)).

2 PROCEDURE IN CRIMINAL CASES: CHILD WITNESSES

1995 ACT, SS 271A AND 271B

Until the Vulnerable Witnesses (Scotland) Act 2004 came into force, any application for the use of special measures could be granted only on cause shown. In deciding that cause had been shown, the court was required to have particular regard to the possible effect on the vulnerable person if required to give evidence without the use of special measures and whether it would be more likely that the witness would be better able to give evidence if such an application were to be granted. Under the new legislation, child witnesses are presumed to be vulnerable purely by reason of their age and they have an automatic entitlement to the benefit of one or more special measures to assist them in giving their evidence. There is no longer any need to show that the quality or coherence of the witness's evidence might be adversely affected by giving evidence in open court in the presence of the accused.

271A Child witnesses

(1) Where a child witness is to give evidence at or for the purposes of a trial, the child witness is entitled, subject to—
  (a) subsections (2) to (13) below, and
  (b) section 271D of this Act,
  to the benefit of one or more of the special measures for the purpose of giving evidence.

(2) A party citing or intending to cite a child witness shall, no later than 14 clear days before the trial diet, lodge with the court a notice (referred to in this Act as a "child witness notice")—
  (a) specifying the special measure or measures which the party considers to be the most appropriate for the purpose of taking the child witness's evidence, or
  (b) if the party considers that the child witness should give evidence without the benefit of any special measure, stating that fact.

(3) A child witness notice shall contain or be accompanied by—
  (a) a summary of any views expressed for the purposes of section 271E(2)(b) of this Act, and
  (b) such other information as may be prescribed by Act of Adjournal.

(4) The court may, on cause shown, allow a child witness notice to be lodged after the time limit specified in subsection (2) above.

(5) The court shall, not later than 7 days after a child witness notice has been lodged, consider the notice in the absence of the parties and, subject to section 271B(3) of this Act—
   (a) in the case of a notice under subsection (2)(a) above—
      (i) if a standard special measure is specified in the notice, make an order authorising the use of that measure for the purpose of taking the child witness's evidence, and
      (ii) if any other special measure is specified in the notice and the court is satisfied on the basis of the notice that it is appropriate to do so, make an order authorising the use of the special measure (in addition to any authorised by virtue of an order under sub-paragraph (i) above) for the purpose of taking the child witness's evidence,
   (b) in the case of a notice under subsection (2)(b) above, if—
      (i) the summary of views accompanying the notice under subsection (3)(a) above indicates that the child witness has expressed a wish to give evidence without the benefit of any special measure, and
      (ii) the court is satisfied on the basis of the notice that it is appropriate to do so,
   make an order authorising the giving of evidence by the child witness without the benefit of any special measure, or
   (c) if—
      (i) paragraph (a)(ii) or (b) above would apply but for the fact that the court is not satisfied as mentioned in that paragraph, or
      (ii) in the case of a notice under subsection (2)(b), the summary of views accompanying the notice under subsection (3)(a) above indicates that the child witness has not expressed a wish to give evidence without the benefit of any special measure,
   make an order that, before the trial diet, there shall be a diet under subsection (9) below and ordain the parties to attend.

(6) Subsection (7) below applies where—
   (a) it appears to the court that a party intends to call a child witness to give evidence at or for the purposes of the trial,
   (b) the party has not lodged a child witness notice in respect of the child witness by the time specified in subsection (2) above, and

> (c) the court has not allowed a child witness notice in respect of the child witness to be lodged after that time under subsection (4) above.

(7) Where this subsection applies, the court shall—
>   (a) order the party to lodge a child witness notice in respect of the child witness by such time as the court may specify, or
>   (b) order that, before the trial diet, there shall be a diet under subsection (9) below and ordain the parties to attend.

(8) On making an order under subsection (5)(c) or (7)(b) above, the court may postpone the trial diet.

(9) At a diet under this subsection, the court, after giving the parties an opportunity to be heard—
>   (a) in a case where any of the standard special measures has been authorised by an order under subsection (5)(a)(i) above, may make an order authorising the use of such further special measure or measures as it considers appropriate for the purpose of taking the child witness's evidence, and
>   (b) in any other case, shall make an order—
>   (i) authorising the use of such special measure or measures as the court considers to be the most appropriate for the purpose of taking the child witness's evidence, or
>   (ii) that the child witness is to give evidence without the benefit of any special measure.

(10) The court may make an order under subsection (9)(b)(ii) above only if satisfied—
>   (a) where the child witness has expressed a wish to give evidence without the benefit of any special measure, that it is appropriate for the child witness so to give evidence, or
>   (b) in any other case, that—
>   (i) the use of any special measure for the purpose of taking the evidence of the child witness would give rise to a significant risk of prejudice to the fairness of the trial or otherwise to the interests of justice, and
>   (ii) that risk significantly outweighs any risk of prejudice to the interests of the child witness if the order is made.

(11) A diet under subsection (9) above may—
>   (a) on the application of the party citing or intending to cite the child witness in respect of whom the diet is to be held, or

> *(b)* of the court's own motion,
> be held in chambers.
>
> *(12)* A diet under subsection (9) above may be conjoined with—
> *(a)* in the case of proceedings in the High Court, a preliminary diet,
> *(b)* in the case of proceedings on indictment in the sheriff court, a first diet,
> *(c)* in the case of summary proceedings, an intermediate diet.
>
> *(13)* A party lodging a child witness notice shall, at the same time, intimate the notice to the other parties to the proceedings.
>
> *(14)* In this section, references to a standard special measure are to any of the following special measures—
> *(a)* the use of a live television link in accordance with section 271J of this Act where the place from which the child witness is to give evidence by means of the link is another part of the court building in which the courtroom is located,
> *(b)* the use of a screen in accordance with section 271K of this Act, and
> *(c)* the use of a supporter in accordance with section 271L of this Act in conjunction with either of the special measures referred to in paragraphs (a) and (b) above.

In any case in which there is a child witness, the party citing the witness must consider at as early a stage as possible which measure or measures would be most appropriate, having taken the views of the witness and his or her parent or parents into account. The provisions are drafted in such a way as to make the granting of authorisation for the use of special measures for child witnesses an administrative process without the need for court hearings or prolonged legal debate. Where standard special measures are requested (live television link or screen with or without the presence of a supporter) they will be granted. The court may order that the child give evidence without the use of special measures only in very limited circumstances.

Section 271A provides that the party who has cited or intends to cite a child witness must lodge a child witness notice with the court. This is irrespective of whether or not it is intended that special measures are to be used. In High Court cases the notice must be lodged no later than 14 clear days before the preliminary hearing; in solemn cases in the sheriff court, no later than 7 clear days before the first diet; and in any other case no later than 14 clear days before the trial diet. The court may, on cause shown, allow a child witness notice to be lodged late. In the majority of, but by no means all, cases, the witness will be cited by the prosecution. The child witness notice must conform to Form 22.1 of the Act of Adjournal (Criminal Procedure Rules) 1996 (SI 1996/513), as amended. It must state the special measure or measures the party considers to be most appropriate for the purpose of taking the child's evidence, or state that the child witness should give evidence without the benefit of any special measure if the party believes that to be the most appropriate course of action. The notice must include or be accompanied by a summary of any views expressed by the witness, and his or her parents or persons with parental responsibilities for the child, unless the parent or person with parental responsibilities is also the accused. If the child is aged 12 or over, then he or she shall be presumed to be of sufficient age and maturity to form a view. Should there be a conflict between the views of the child and the parents, then the views of the child are to be given greater weight. Where the child has expressed the wish to testify without the use of special measures, the court must be satisfied that it is appropriate for him or her to do so. It is expected that in most cases the court will respect the wishes of the child witness unless it is clear that he or she is being thoroughly intransigent in declining the use of special measures.

The notice must be intimated to the other parties to the proceedings. Child witness notices must be considered by the court in the absence of the parties not more than 7 days after they have been lodged. The court must make its decision based solely on the information contained in the notice. Where a standard special measure (live television link or screen with or without the presence of a support person) is specified in the notice, the party citing does not require to state reasons for the choice and the court must make an order authorising the use of the stated measure or measures. The court has no discretion to refuse the use of the standard special measure or measures requested by the party citing the witness or to authorise the use of its own preferred one.

Where other special measures are specified (the use of a supporter, the taking of evidence by a commissioner, evidence in chief in the form of a prior statement or the use of a live television link from a remote location), if the court "is satisfied on the basis of the notice" that it is appropriate to do so, it must make an order authorising the use of that special measure, in addition, where appropriate, to any standard special measures authorised under s 271A(5)(a)(i). The party citing the witness must set out in Form 22.1 the reasons that the other special measure or measures are considered the most appropriate in the circumstances. Care must be taken to include as much information as is necessary to enable the court to make an informed decision. If the summary of views contained in the notice indicates that the child witness has expressed a wish to give evidence without the benefit of special measures and the court is satisfied on the basis of the reasons set out in Form 22.1 that it is appropriate to do so, the court must make an order authorising the child to give evidence without the use of special measures.

However, if the court is not satisfied on the basis of the notice that the use of another special measure is appropriate, or where the child has not expressed a wish to give evidence without the benefit of any special measure, the court must make an order under s 271A(5A). Such orders can appoint that the child witness notice be dealt with at the preliminary hearing in High Court cases, or the first diet in solemn cases in the sheriff court if they are yet to be held, or in any other case at a diet before the trial diet, and ordain the parties to attend. The accused is present at such hearings but the witnesses are not.

Section 271A is drafted so as to ensure that even if the party citing has omitted to lodge a child witness notice timeously, the question of special measures will not be overlooked. In cases in which the court has not permitted the notice to be lodged late, the court may order the party to lodge the notice by such time as the court specifies or, if it does not so order, make an order appointing a diet to be held before the trial diet and requiring the parties to attend (s 271A(7)). The diet may take place in chambers. At the hearing, after the parties have been given an opportunity to be heard, the court has three options.

- If standard special measures have already been granted, the court may authorise the use of such further special measures as it considers appropriate for the purpose of taking the child witness's evidence.

- In any other case the court must authorise the use of such measure or measures as the court considers most appropriate for the purposes of taking the child's evidence; or

- order that the child is to give evidence without the benefit of any special measure.

The court may make an order that the child is to give evidence without the use of special measures only where:

- the child has expressed a wish to give evidence without special measures and the court is satisfied that it is appropriate for the child to do so;

- the use of any special measure would give rise to a significant risk of prejudice to the fairness of the trial or otherwise to the interests of justice and that risk significantly outweighs any risk of prejudice to the interests of the child witness if the order is made.

The wording of the section is not particularly easy to follow, but it is suggested that the court may refuse authorisation only if it is satisfied that there is no special measure, among the several available that could be used, that would not give rise to significant risk of prejudice to the fairness of the trial. It is difficult to envisage the practical circumstances in which such a risk might arise. All of the measures, most of which were already available under statute or at common law before the 2004 Act was passed, ensure that the accused can see and hear the witness while he or she testifies. The witness can also be cross-examined. If, for example, objections were raised that the material contained in a prior statement had been obtained as a result of suggestion and leading questions, then that might meet the criteria set out in s 271A(10), but then it would be open to the court to authorise the use of a less potentially controversial special measure such as the use of the live television link or a screen.

Only the court may order that a hearing take place. There is no mechanism for any other parties to proceedings to raise the question of significant risk of prejudice to the trial. Other parties are dependent on the court first holding that it is not satisfied on the basis of the notice that the use of other special measures is appropriate before they can have the opportunity to be heard on the matter. This should not cause any difficulties where standard special measures are sought. This is because the child is a vulnerable witness solely by virtue of his or her age and has an automatic entitlement at least to standard special measures. However, if authorisation for the use of other special measures is sought and granted administratively, other parties to proceedings have no means of persuading the court that its decision may be wrong, unless the party raises the matter at a preliminary hearing in the High Court (s 72(6)(b)) or a first diet in the sheriff court (s 71(2)), as either a preliminary issue such as an objection to the admissibility of any evidence (s 79(2)(b)(iv)) or any other matter not otherwise mentioned in s 79(2)(b) which could in the opinion of the party be resolved with advantage before the trial (s 79(2)(b)(vi)).

By making compulsory the submission of a child witness notice and the process of granting authorisation to use standard special measures an administrative matter, rather than an issue to be resolved by legal debate, there is a genuine chance that the use of special measures will come to be viewed as the norm in child witness situations, that child witnesses will be reassured that they can prepare themselves for court in the knowledge that they will be granted assistance to give their evidence should they wish it and that it will be the help they consider would best suit them. The use of special measures will not necessarily ensure that the witness will be able to give evidence without distress. However, the provisions of s 271A must improve the chances of child witnesses being able to give coherent, comprehensible evidence so that the court or the jury can assess their credibility and reliability as effectively as possible. Furthermore, as every child is entitled to special measures the danger is removed that a jury might draw an adverse inference from their use as to the accused's guilt even in the face of directions from the judge to the contrary.

Further special provision for child witnesses under the age of 12 (1995 Act, s 271B)

271B Further special provision for child witnesses under the age of 12

(1) This section applies where a child witness—

  (a) is to give evidence at, or for the purposes of, a trial in respect of any offence specified in subsection (2) below, and

  (b) is under the age of 12 on the date of commencement of the proceedings in which the trial is being or to be held.

(2) The offences referred to in subsection (1)(a) above are—

  (a) murder,

  (b) culpable homicide,

  (c) any offence to which section 288C of this Act applies,

  (d) any offence which involves an assault on, or injury or a threat of injury to, any person (including any offence involving neglect or ill-treatment of, or other cruelty to, a child),

  (e) abduction, and

  (f) plagium.

(3) Where this section applies, the court shall not make an order under section 271A or 271D of this Act which has the effect of requiring the child witness to be present in the court-room or any part of the court building in which the court-room is located for the purpose of giving evidence unless satisfied—

  (a) where the child witness has expressed a wish to be so present for the purposes of giving evidence, that it is appropriate for the child witness to be so present for that purpose, or

  (b) in any other case, that—

    (i) the taking of the evidence of the child witness without the child witness being so present would give rise to a significant risk of prejudice to the fairness of the trial or otherwise to the interests of justice, and

    (ii) that risk significantly outweighs any risk of prejudice to the interests of the child witness if the order is made.

Section 271B makes additional provision for child witnesses who are under the age of 12 on the date that proceedings commence and who are to give evidence in a trial for an offence specified in s 271B(2). These offences are: murder; culpable homicide; those statutory and common law offences specified in s 288C of the 1995 Act; any offence involving an assault or injury to any person including any offence involving neglect or ill treatment of, or other cruelty to, a child; abduction; and *plagium*. The fact that the witness was under the age of 12 when proceedings commenced must be included in the child witness notice. Section 271B states that the court will not make an order authorising the use of special measures which would have the effect of the child giving their evidence in the courtroom or any part of the building in which the courtroom is situated, unless the child has expressed a wish to be present in the courtroom or court building and the court is satisfied that it is appropriate for the child witness to be present for that purpose, or in any other case if satisfied that the taking of the evidence without the child being present would "give rise to a significant risk of prejudice to the fairness of the trial or otherwise to the interests of justice and that risk significantly outweighs the any risk of prejudice to the interests of the child witness if the order is made". The special measures which enable the child to give evidence in this way are the taking of evidence by a commissioner or the use of a live television link from a remote location. If an order is made under s 271B(3)(b) which has the effect of the child giving evidence in the court building, the child witness would still be entitled at least to the use of standard special measures under s 271A.

Section 271B(3)(b)(i) and (ii) *inter alia* require the court to balance the interests of the witness against the risk of possible prejudice to the accused. This is potentially the most controversial aspect of the 2004 Act. During the passage of the Bill, it was stated to the Justice 2 Committee that the subsections were worded so as to remind sheriffs and judges that the expectation was that they should grant authorisation for the use of special measures and that both the interests of the accused and the interests of the witnesses should be the paramount consideration for the court. Quite how this could logically be achieved was not explained. It appears that the subsections are intended to ensure that the requirement to comply with the accused's right to a fair trial in terms of Art 6 of ECHR is balanced against the witness's competing rights under Arts 3 and 8. However, the inclusion of this provision may be subject to challenge. As drafted, it appears to permit a court to agree that there is a significant risk of prejudice to the fairness of the trial if the use of special measures is authorised, but because that risk is equivalent to, or less than, the risk of prejudice to the interests of the witness, or the risk of prejudice to the fairness of the trial is outweighed by the risk of prejudice to the interests of the witness, but not significantly, then the court ought still to authorise the use of special measures. It remains to be seen how the courts would deal with any challenge to this aspect of the legislation. However, in *Clark* v *HM Advocate* 2004 SLT 9, which was concerned with whether there had been a breach of the appellant's right to a fair hearing within a reasonable time, it was held that it was not appropriate for the court to "embark on a balancing act in the course of which any prejudice sustained was balanced against the 'rights of the victim' should the case not proceed" (per Lord Kirkwood at 13). It seems unlikely in the face of a challenge that the court would hold that these provisions, which in effect sanction an unfair trial in order to maintain a balance with the rights of witnesses, were compatible with Convention rights.

3 PROCEDURE IN CRIMINAL CASES: ADULT VULNERABLE WITNESSES

1995 ACT, S 271C

While child witnesses now have an automatic entitlement to the use of standard special measures should they wish it, adult vulnerable witnesses continue to have a discretionary entitlement to the use of special measures. The new provisions on adult vulnerable witnesses are intended to be more inclusive and flexible than under the previous legislation and will result in there being many more witnesses who will be eligible for consideration for special measures than before.

271C Vulnerable witnesses other than child witnesses

(1) This section applies where a party citing or intending to cite a person (other than a child witness) to give evidence at, or for the purposes of, a trial (such a person being referred to in this section as "the witness") considers—
  (a) that the witness is likely to be a vulnerable witness, and
  (b) that a special measure or combination of special measures ought to be used for the purpose of taking the witness's evidence.

(2) Where this section applies, the party citing or intending to cite the witness shall, not later than 14 clear days before the trial diet, make an application (referred to as a "vulnerable witness application") to the court for an order authorising the use of one or more of the special measures for the purpose of taking the witness's evidence.

(3) A vulnerable witness application shall—
  (a) specify the special measure or measures which the party making the application considers to be the most appropriate for the purpose of taking the evidence of the witness to whom the application relates, and
  (b) contain or be accompanied by—
    (i) a summary of any views expressed for the purposes of section 271E(2)(b) of this Act, and
    (ii) such other information as may be prescribed by Act of Adjournal.

(4) The court may, on cause shown, allow a vulnerable witness application to be made after the time limit specified in subsection (2) above.

(5) The court shall, not later than 7 days after a vulnerable witness application is made to it, consider the application in the absence of the parties and—

    (a) make an order authorising the use of the special measure or measures specified in the application if satisfied on the basis of the application that—

        (i) the witness in respect of whom the application is made is a vulnerable witness,

        (ii) the special measures or measures specified in the application are the most appropriate for the purpose of taking the witness's evidence, and

        (iii) it is appropriate to do so after having complied with the duty in subsection (8) below, or

    (b) if not satisfied as mentioned in paragraph (a) above, order that, before the trial diet, there shall be a diet under subsection (7) below and ordain the parties to attend.

(6) On making an order under subsection (5)(b) above, the court may postpone the trial diet.

(7) At a diet under this subsection, the court may—

    (a) after giving the parties an opportunity to be heard, and

    (b) if satisfied that the witness in respect of whom the application is made is a vulnerable witness,

make an order authorising the use of such special measure or measures as the court considers to be the most appropriate for the purpose of taking the witness's evidence.

(8) In deciding whether to make an order under subsection (5)(a) or (7) above, the court shall—

    (a) have regard to—

        (i) the possible effect on the witness if required to give evidence without the benefit of any special measure, and

        (ii) whether it is likely that the witness would be better able to give evidence with the benefit of a special measure, and

    (b) take into account the matters specified in subsection (2)(a) to (f) of section 271 of this Act.

(9) A diet under subsection (7) above may—

    (a) on the application of the party citing or intending to cite the witness in respect of whom the diet is to be held, or

    (b) of the court's own motion,

be held in chambers.

(10) A diet under subsection (7) above may be conjoined with—

    (a) in the case of proceedings in the High Court, a preliminary diet,

> *(b) in the case of proceedings on indictment in the sheriff court, a first diet,*
>
> *(c) in the case of summary proceedings, an intermediate diet.*
>
> *(11) A party making a vulnerable witness application shall, at the same time, intimate the application to the other parties to the proceedings.*

The procedure to be followed when an adult vulnerable witness is to be cited is set out in the 1995 Act, s 271C. As with child witnesses, responsibility for identifying that an adult witness may be vulnerable and that one or more special measures ought to be used for the purpose of taking the witness's evidence lies with the party citing or intending to cite the witness. However, instead of lodging a notice, the citing party must by the required time make a vulnerable witness application to the court seeking an order permitting the use of one or more special measures in respect of that witness's evidence. The required time is no later than 14 clear days before the preliminary hearing, first diet or trial diet.

The application must conform to Form 22.1A and be lodged with the court (Act of Adjournal (Criminal Procedure) Rules 1996, r 22.1A). It must specify the name and date of birth of the witness, set out the reasons for considering that the witness is likely to be a vulnerable witness, the measure or measures which the citing party considers most appropriate for the purpose of taking the evidence and the reasons for its view, and must include a summary of the views of the witness and any other information considered relevant to the application.

A copy of the application must be served on the other parties to proceedings. When an application is submitted to the court, the clerk of court notes the date and time of receipt on it and places it before a judge or sheriff in chambers (r 22.2(1)). Within 7 days after lodging the application, or at least 2 days before the first diet or preliminary hearing, whichever is earlier, the citing party must also lodge a certificate of intimation on other parties to the proceedings with the clerk of court (r 22.1(2)).

Applications must be considered by the court in chambers not later than 7 days after being lodged. The court must make an order authorising the use of the measures if it "is satisfied on the basis of the application" that several matters have been established. As a first step, the court must be satisfied on the basis of the information contained in the notice that the witness is a vulnerable witness as now defined in s 271(1)(b)(i) or (ii). Therefore it is incumbent on the party citing or considering citing the witness to explain clearly the reason or reasons for the witness's vulnerability. The next stage for the court is to consider whether it agrees that the special measure is or measures are the most appropriate for the purpose of taking the witness's evidence. Again, this will depend upon the citing party making a convincing case in the application for the use of the particular measure or measures. The views of the witness as to which measure would best suit him or her will also inform the decision of the court. Finally, the court must be satisfied that it is appropriate to make the order having complied with its duty to have regard to *both* the possible effect on the witness if required to give evidence without the benefit of any special measure *and* whether it is likely that the witness would be better able to give evidence with the benefit of a special measure. In reaching a decision on both of these issues, the court must take into account the issues set out in s 271(2)(a)–(f). (See pp 7–8 and 11–12.) All the conditions in s 271C(5)(a) must be met before the court can make an order authorising the use of special measures. The court may grant authorisation for the use of special measures administratively. However, if it is not satisfied on the basis of the notice that the conditions set out in s 271C(5)(a)(i), (ii) and (iii), the court may not refuse an application outright without first hearing from parties.

If the court is not satisfied on the basis of the application that all of the qualifying conditions have been met, it must make an order under s 271C(5A). Such an order is to the effect that in High Court or sheriff and jury cases, the vulnerable witness application be disposed of at the preliminary hearing or the first diet where those diets have not yet been disposed of, or in any other case fixing a diet to be held in advance of the trial diet and ordaining parties to attend. If necessary, the court may postpone the trial diet in order to hold the subsection (7) diet. However, as the ensuing delay in giving evidence caused by adjourning the trial would no doubt cause distress and anxiety to the witness, it is suggested that postponements should be avoided whenever possible.

At a subsection (7) diet, if, after hearing from the parties, the court is satisfied that the witness meets the criteria of vulnerability, it may make an order authorising the use of those special measures it considers most appropriate for the purpose of taking the witness's evidence. In reaching that decision the court takes into account the same criteria as when considering an application in chambers. The hearing, if held on its own, may be held in chambers. If conjoined with a preliminary diet in the High Court or a first diet or intermediate diet in the sheriff court, it takes place in open court. The accused is present at such hearings. Witnesses in the case are not present.

Although the legislation no longer states that vulnerable witness applications may be granted only on cause shown, in practical terms, the party citing the witness must show that there is a good reason for the court to grant authorisation for the use of special measures. Therefore, it is very important that the vulnerable witness application sets out, clearly and in detail, sufficient relevant information and sound reasons to enable the court to reach a decision on the basis of the notice. Citing parties must be adept at identifying potentially vulnerable adult witnesses at the earliest opportunity and providing as much supporting evidence as possible in applications and accompanying reports to satisfy the conditions set out in s 271C(5)(a). Under the previous legislation, it became the practice for the citing party to obtain supporting reports from social workers, medical practitioners or other relevant persons who could explain to the court the reasons for the witness's vulnerability and the impact on him and the quality of his evidence of giving evidence without special measures. It would seem sensible for citing parties to continue with this practice.

In preparing a vulnerable witness application, the citing party must make it clear to the witness that the decision to grant or refuse authorisation for special measures rests with the court. The citing party will also require to explain that any information contained in the application or in the supporting documents will be disclosed to the other parties and could be used by the defence to the witness's disadvantage. The autonomy of witnesses should be respected and it should not be assumed that all potentially vulnerable adult witnesses will choose to seek authorisation for the use of special measures once furnished with the information to make an informed choice.

The terms of s 271C(5)(a) imply that applications are intended to be considered in chambers and granted as a matter of course. However, as explained above, the matters to be taken into account by the court set out in ss 271(1) and (2) and 271C(8)(a) and (b) give the court considerable scope to refuse to make the order at first instance and order that a hearing be held. Other than at a hearing ordered under s 271C(5A), other parties to proceedings have no *locus* to be heard on whether the witness is vulnerable and in need of special measures. Since a preliminary hearing or first diet must take place in all solemn cases, it is possible that the courts will adopt the practice of ordering hearings to dispose of vulnerable witness applications in the majority of cases. The courts may be unlikely, at least initially, to authorise the use of special measures simply on the basis of the averments in a vulnerable witness application and *ex parte* supporting statements, especially if the reasons for making the application include fear and distress in connection with giving evidence at the trial caused by alleged intimidation of the witness by the accused or an associate of the accused.

Even if an application is granted in chambers, it is not immediately obvious that the ensuing authorisation to use special measures would necessarily prejudice the accused's right to a fair trial. The trial proceedings themselves would still take place in the presence of the accused, he or she would be able to see and hear the witness, and the witness would be subject to cross-examination. The accused would be able to challenge the credibility and reliability of the witness and to appeal against conviction. However, it is suggested that the most practical way of ensuring that any concerns about the vulnerability of the witness or the appropriateness of the use of special measures are heard and taken into account would be for the court to declare itself not satisfied on the basis of the application and to fix a hearing in all but the most obvious cases and certainly where it is averred that vulnerability arises due to fear and distress in connection with giving evidence.

If the court fixes a hearing then, having heard parties, the court may grant or refuse authorisation for the use of special measures. There is a limited right to appeal decisions made in respect of adult vulnerable witnesses at preliminary hearings or first diets under the 1995 Act, s 74. That right does not extend to challenging the issue of vulnerability but it does permit a review of the court's decision to hold itself satisfied that the conditions in s 271C(5)(a)(ii) and (iii) have been met.

Orders under s 271C are signed by the clerk of court. Those made in chambers are intimated to all parties unless the parties were present at a hearing at which the order was made. An order for the disposal of an application at the preliminary or first diet must where the accused is in custody be intimated to the governor of the institution in which he or she is detained (r 22.3A).

4 REVIEW OF SPECIAL MEASURES, APPLICATION TO THE ACCUSED, SUPPLEMENTARY AND SAVING PROVISIONS AND APPLICATION OF VULNERABLE WITNESS PROVISIONS TO PROCEEDINGS IN THE DISTRICT COURT

1995 ACT, SS 271D–271G AND S 288G

271D Review of arrangements for vulnerable witnesses

(1) In any case in which a person who is giving or is to give evidence at or for the purposes of the trial (referred to in this section as the "witness") is or appears to the court to be a vulnerable witness, the court may at any stage in the proceedings (whether before or after the commencement of the trial or before or after the witness has begun to give evidence)—

(a) on the application of the party citing or intending to cite the witness, or

(b) of its own motion,

review the current arrangements for taking the witness's evidence and, after giving the parties an opportunity to be heard, make an order under subsection (2) below.

(2) The order which may be made under this subsection is—

(a) where the current arrangements for taking the witness's evidence include the use of a special measure or combination of special measures authorised by an order under section 271A or 271C of this Act or under this subsection (referred to as the "earlier order"), an order varying or revoking the earlier order, or

(b) where the current arrangements for taking the witness's evidence do not include any special measure, an order authorising the use of such special measure or measures as the court considers most appropriate for the purpose of taking the witness's evidence.

(3) An order under subsection (2)(a) above varying an earlier order may—

(a) add to or substitute for any special measure authorised by the earlier order such other special measure as the court considers most appropriate for the purpose of taking the witness's evidence, or *(b)* *where the earlier order authorises the use of a combination of special measures for that purpose, delete any of the special measures so authorised.*

 (4) *The court may make an order under subsection (2)(a) above revoking an earlier order only if satisfied—*

   (a) *where the witness has expressed a wish to give or, as the case may be, continue to give evidence without the benefit of any special measure, that it is appropriate for the witness so to give evidence, or*

   (b) *in any other case, that—*

     (i) *the use, or continued use, of the special measure or measures authorised by the earlier order for the purpose of taking the witness's evidence would give rise to a significant risk of prejudice to the fairness of the trial or otherwise to the interests of justice, and*

     (ii) *that risk significantly outweighs any risk of prejudice to the interests of the witness if the order is made.*

 (5) *Subsection (8) of section 271C of this Act applies to the making of an order under subsection (2)(b) of this section as it applies to the making of an order under subsection (5)(a) or (7) of that section but as if the references to the witness were to the witness within the meaning of this section.*

 (6) *In this section, "current arrangements" means the arrangements in place at the time the review under this section is begun.*

Review of special measures

The court may review at any stage in the proceedings the current arrangements for taking the vulnerable witness's evidence. A review can take place before or after the trial has commenced or before or after the witness has begun to give evidence. It may do so on the motion of the party citing the witness or on its own motion and, having given the parties the opportunity to be heard, may make an order varying or revoking an earlier order to authorise the use of a special measure or measures, or authorising the use of special measures where no such order already exists. An order may substitute one measure that is considered more appropriate for an existing one or may add a special measure. Where a combination of measures has previously been ordered, any of the measures may be deleted. Applications may be made orally or in writing by minute in Form 22.4 (1996 Rules, r 22.4) and must set out the reasons for review and the nature of the order sought. The minute must be lodged with the court and served on all other parties to proceedings by the minuter. There is no scope for any other party to proceedings to seek a review of arrangements. The court may revoke the earlier order only in limited circumstances. It may do so in cases where the witness has expressed a wish to give or continue to give evidence without the use of special measures but the court must be satisfied that it is appropriate for the witness so to give evidence. In any other case it must be satisfied that the use or continued use of special measures would give rise to a significant risk of prejudice to the fairness of the trial or otherwise to the interests of justice and that risk would significantly outweigh any risk of prejudice to the interests of the witness. The review provisions therefore offer no means for other parties to proceedings to request a review. There is no scope for an appeal of a decision made in respect of a review under s 271D.

271F The accused

(1) For the purposes of the application of subsection (1) of section 271 of this Act to the accused (where the accused is giving or is to give evidence at or for the purposes of the trial), subsection (2) of that section shall have effect as if—

  (a) for paragraph (c) there were substituted—

    "(c) whether the accused is to be legally represented at the trial and, if not, the accused's entitlement to be so legally represented,", and

  (b) for paragraph (e) there were substituted—

    "(e) any behaviour towards the accused on the part of—

      (i) any co-accused or any person who is likely to be a co-accused in the proceedings,

      (ii) any witness or any person who is likely to be a witness in the proceedings, or

      (iii) members of the family or associates of any of the persons mentioned in sub-paragraphs (i) and (ii) above.".

(2) Where, if the accused were to give evidence at or for the purposes of the trial, he would be a child witness—

  (a) section 271A of this Act shall apply in relation to the accused subject to the following modifications—

    (i) references to a child witness (except in the phrase "child witness notice") shall be read as if they were references to the accused,

    (ii) references to the party citing or intending to cite a child witness shall be read as if they were references to the accused, and

    (iii) subsection (6) shall have effect as if for paragraph (a) there were substituted—

      "(a) it appears to the court that the accused, if he were to give evidence at or for the purposes of the trial, would be a child witness,", and

(b) section 271B of this Act shall apply in relation to the accused as if—

(i) for subsection (1) there were substituted—

"(1) This section applies where the accused—

(a) if he were to give evidence at or for the purposes of the trial would be a child witness, and

(b) is under the age of 12 on the date of commencement of the proceedings.", and

(ii) in subsection (3), references to the child witness were references to the accused.

(3) Subsection (4) below applies where the accused—

(a) considers that, if he were to give evidence at or for the purposes of the trial, he would be a vulnerable witness other than a child witness, and

(b) has not decided to give evidence without the benefit of any special measures.

(4) Where this subsection applies, subsections (2) to (11) of section 271C of this Act shall apply in relation to the accused subject to the following modifications—

(a) references to the witness shall be read as if they were references to the accused,

(b) references to the party citing or intending to cite the witness shall be read as if they were references to the accused, and

(c) in subsection (8)(b), the reference to subsection (2)(a) to (f) of section 271 of this Act shall be read as if it were a reference to that subsection as modified by subsection (1) above.

(5) Section 271D of this Act shall apply in any case where it appears to the court that the accused, if he were to give evidence at or for the purposes of the trial, would be a vulnerable witness as it applies in the case referred to in subsection (1) of that section but subject to the following modifications—

(a) references to the witness shall be read as if they were references to the accused,

(b) references to the party citing or intending to cite the witness shall be read as if they were references to the accused.

(6) Where the witness within the meaning of section 271E of this Act is the accused, that section shall have effect in relation to the witness as if—

(a) in subsection (1), paragraph (a) were omitted, and

(b) in subsection (2), the words "The party or, as the case may be," were omitted.

(7) Section 271M of this Act shall have effect, where the vulnerable witness is the accused, as if the reference in subsection (2) to the party citing the vulnerable witness were a reference to the accused.

(8) The following provisions of this Act shall not apply in relation to a vulnerable witness who is the accused—
(a) section 271H(1)(c),
(b) section 271I(3).

Section 271F provides for the accused to make use of special measures when giving evidence in the event that he or she is deemed to be vulnerable. It makes modifications to sections 271, 271A, 271B and 271C so as to enable them to apply to the accused. The factors to be taken into account in assessing vulnerability in an adult accused include whether the accused is to be legally represented and his or her entitlement to be legally represented, and any behaviour towards the accused by any co-accused, witness or family member or associate of the co-accused or witness. Form 22.1 is used for notices for child accused who are to give evidence and Form 22.1A is used in applications for adult accused. The accused is not entitled to the use of screens as a special measure.

271E Vulnerable witnesses: supplementary provision

(1) Subsection (2) below applies where—
(a) a party is considering for the purposes of a child witness notice or a vulnerable witness application which of the special measures is or are the most appropriate for the purpose of taking the evidence of the person to whom the notice or application relates, or
(b) the court is making an order under section 271A(5)(a)(ii) or (b) or (9), 271C or 271D of this Act.

(2) The party or, as the case may be, the court shall—
(a) have regard to the best interests of the witness, and
(b) take account of any views expressed by—
(i) the witness (having regard, where the witness is a child witness, to the witness's age and maturity), and
(ii) where the witness is a child witness, the witness's parent (except where the parent is the accused).

(3) For the purposes of subsection (2)(b) above, where the witness is a child witness—
(a) the witness shall be presumed to be of sufficient age and maturity to form a view if aged 12 or older, and
(b) in the event that any views expressed by the witness are inconsistent with any views expressed by the witness's parent, the views of the witness shall be given greater weight.

(4) In this section—

> *"parent", in relation to a child witness, means any person having parental responsibilities within the meaning of section 1(3) of the Children (Scotland) Act 1995 (c. 36) in relation to the child witness,*
> *"the witness" means—*
>> *(a) in the case referred to in subsection (1)(a) above, the person to whom the notice or application relates,*
>> *(b) in the case referred to in subsection (1)(b) above, the person to whom the order would relate.*

The first provisions authorising the use of special measures were contained in the Law Reform (Miscellaneous Provisions) (Scotland) Act 1990, ss 56–58 and the Prisoners and Criminal Proceedings (Scotland) Act 1993, ss 33–35 and placed no obligation on the court or the party citing the witness to ascertain the views of the child witness. Such an omission cast doubt on the Government's commitment to the United Nations Convention on the Rights of the Child ratified by the United Kingdom in 1989, Art 12 of which grants children the opportunity to express their views "in any judicial or administrative proceedings affecting them". An evaluation of the operation of the first special measures was critical of this, noting that many of the child witnesses interviewed had wanted to be consulted on their wishes as they felt this made them feel more in control of events (K Murray, *Live Television Link: An Evaluation of its Use by Child Witnesses in Scottish Criminal Trials* (Scottish Office, 1995)). When the legislation on special measures was consolidated into s 271 of the Criminal Procedure (Scotland) Act 1995 (s 271(7)(c)) for the first time it included the views of the child as a factor to be taken into account by the court when considering an application for the authorisation of special measures.

Section 271E obliges the party citing the witness (whether a child or an adult), or the court, to have regard to the best interests of the witness and to take account of any views expressed by the witness. Where the witness is a child, the age and maturity of the child and the views of the child's parent, except where the parent is the accused, are also to be taken into account. A witness aged 12 or older is presumed to be of sufficient age and maturity to form a view. In the event that the views of the child and the parent do not coincide, the views of the child are to be given precedence. The section appears to permit the citing party or the court not to act on the views of the witness if it considers that to do so would be in the best interests of the witness. A difficult teenage child witness might state that he or she did not wish to use special measures in circumstances in which it would be obvious to his or her parents, the citing party and the court that it was in their own best interests to use special measures. In terms of ss 271A(5)(b)(ii) and 271B(3)(a), the court should make an order to the effect that the child is to give evidence without the benefit of special measures, or requiring a child witness under the age of 12 to give evidence in the courtroom or court building in which the court is situated, only where the child has expressed a wish to do so and the court is satisfied on the basis of the child witness notice that it is appropriate to do so.

271G Saving provision

> *Nothing in sections 271A to 271F of this Act affects any power or duty which a court has otherwise than by virtue of those sections to make or authorise any special arrangements for taking the evidence of any person.*

Section 271G preserves the existing common law powers of the court to authorise the use of special measures for the taking of a vulnerable witness's evidence. In *Hampson and Others* v *HM Advocate* 2003 SCCR 13 the court rejected the argument of counsel for the accused that the version of s 271 in force at that time had superseded any common law powers that the courts might once have had to authorise the use of special measures.

10 Application of vulnerable witnesses provisions to proceedings in the district court

> *After section 288F of the 1995 Act (as inserted by section 6 of this Act) there is inserted—*
> "Application of vulnerable witnesses provisions to proceedings in the district court

> **288G Application of vulnerable witnesses provisions to proceedings in the district court**

> *(1) The Scottish Ministers may by order made by statutory instrument provide for any of sections—*
> *(a) 271 to 271M,*
> *(b) 288E, and*
> *(c) 288F,*
> *of this Act to apply, subject to such modifications (if any) as may be specified in the order, to proceedings in the district court.*

> *(2) An order under subsection (1) may—*
> *(a) make such incidental, supplemental, consequential, transitional, transitory or saving provision as the Scottish Ministers think necessary or expedient,*
> *(b) make different provision for different district courts or descriptions of district court or different proceedings or types of proceedings,*
> *(c) modify any enactment.*

(3) An order under this section shall not be made unless a draft of the statutory instrument containing the order has been laid before, and approved by resolution of, the Scottish Parliament.".

Section 10 of the 2004 Act inserts s 288G into the 1995 Act. It permits Scottish Ministers by order made by statutory instrument to apply any of the vulnerable witness provisions to proceedings in the district court. At present, if a vulnerable witness is to give evidence in proceedings in the district court, it is not possible for the witness to have the benefit of statutory special measures. There is no particular reason why the measures should not apply to district court cases, although some concerns were voiced during the passage of the Bill that the measures could be extended to the district court without the matter requiring to be further debated by the Scottish Parliament.

However, no district court premises have, as yet, been suitably equipped to enable vulnerable witnesses to give evidence there with the benefit of special measures. It appears that the decision not to include district court cases within the ambit of the 2004 Act was taken on economic grounds. Such an omission is likely to cause practical difficulties to arise only where child or vulnerable adult witnesses are cited for the defence in district court cases. In cases in which the witness is required for the prosecution, the Crown Office and Procurator Fiscal Service should be aware of the circumstances of the witness and ought therefore to ensure that proceedings are taken in the sheriff court where the use of special measures is permitted. In cases where the particular court is not sufficiently equipped, an order can be made to transfer the case to another court within the sheriffdom that is suitably equipped.

5 MISCELLANEOUS AMENDMENTS TO EXISTING CRIMINAL JUSTICE LEGISLATION

The remainder of Pt 1 of the 2004 Act inserts additions and makes amendments to the Criminal Procedure (Scotland) Act 1995 and the Criminal Justice (Scotland) Act 2003. Those parts of the 2004 Act amending provisions which related to preliminary diets in the High Court were themselves amended by the Criminal Procedure (Amendment) (Scotland) Act 2004 before the Vulnerable Witnesses (Scotland) Act 2004 had itself come into force.

PRE-TRIAL CONSIDERATIONS (2004 ACT, S 2)

2 Consideration before the trial of matters relating to vulnerable witnesses

(1) In section 71 (first diet of proceedings on indictment in the sheriff court) of the 1995 Act—
(a) after subsection (1) there is inserted—
"(1A) At a first diet, the court shall also—
  (a) ascertain whether subsection (1B) below applies to any person who is to give evidence at or for the purposes of the trial or to the accused, and
  (b) if so, consider whether it should make an order under section 271A(7) or 271D(2) of this Act in relation to the person or, as the case may be, the accused.
(1B) This subsection applies—
  (a) to a person who is to give evidence at or for the purposes of the trial if that person is, or is likely to be, a vulnerable witness,
  (b) to the accused if, were he to give evidence at or for the purposes of the trial, he would be, or would be likely to be, a vulnerable witness.",
(b) in subsection (2), after "(1)" there is inserted "and (1A)", and
(c) in subsection (3), after "(1)" where it first occurs there is inserted ", (1A)".

(2) In section 73 (procedure at preliminary diets in the High Court) of the 1995 Act—
(a) after subsection (3) there is inserted—

"(3A) At a preliminary diet, the court shall also—
  (a) ascertain whether subsection (3B) below applies to any person who is to give evidence at or for the purposes of the trial or to the accused, and
  (b) if so, consider whether it should make an order under section 271A(7) or 271D(2) of this Act in relation to the person or, as the case may be, the accused.

(3B) This subsection applies—
  (a) to a person who is to give evidence at or for the purposes of the trial if that person is, or is likely to be, a vulnerable witness,
  (b) to the accused if, were he to give evidence at or for the purposes of the trial, he would be, or would be likely to be, a vulnerable witness.", and

(b) in subsection (4), for "under subsection (3)" there is substituted "or consider under subsection (3) or (3A)".

(3) After section 73 of the 1995 Act there is inserted—

"73A Consideration of matters relating to vulnerable witnesses where no preliminary diet is ordered

(1) Where, in a case which is to be tried in the High Court, no preliminary diet is ordered, the court shall, at the trial diet before the first witness is sworn—
  (a) ascertain whether subsection (2) below applies to any person who is to give evidence at or for the purposes of the trial or to the accused, and
  (b) if so, consider whether it should make an order under section 271A(7) or 271D(2) of this Act in relation to the person or, as the case may be, to the accused.

(2) This subsection applies—
  (a) to a person who is to give evidence at or for the purposes of the trial if that person is, or is likely to be, a vulnerable witness,
  (b) to the accused if, were he to give evidence at or for the purposes of the trial, he would be, or would be likely to be, a vulnerable witness.

(3) At the trial diet, the court may ask the prosecutor and the accused any question in connection with any matter which it is required to ascertain or consider under subsection (1) above.".

(4) In section 74 (appeals in connection with preliminary diets) of the 1995 Act, in subsection (2), after paragraph (a) there is inserted—
  "(aa) may not be taken against a decision taken by virtue of—
      (i) in the case of a first diet, section 71(1A),
      (ii) in the case of a preliminary diet, section 73(3A),
    of this Act;".

(5) In section 148 (intermediate diet in summary proceedings) of the 1995 Act—

(a) after subsection (1) there is inserted—

"(1A) At an intermediate diet in summary proceedings in the sheriff court, the court shall also—

> *(a) ascertain whether subsection (1B) below applies to any person who is to give evidence at or for the purposes of the trial or to the accused, and*

> *(b) if so, consider whether it should make an order under section 271A(7) or 271D(2) of this Act in relation to the person or, as the case may be, the accused.*

(1B) This subsection applies—

> *(a) to a person who is to give evidence at or for the purposes of the trial if that person is, or is likely to be, a vulnerable witness,*

> *(b) to the accused if, were he to give evidence at or for the purposes of the trial, he would be, or would be likely to be, a vulnerable witness.", and*

(b) in subsection (4), at the end there is inserted "or for the purpose of ascertaining or considering any matter mentioned in subsection (1A) above".

Section 2 amends ss 71 and 148 of the 1995 Act to take account of the duty of the court at first diet and intermediate diet to establish whether there are any vulnerable witnesses in the case and whether it should make an order under ss 271A(7) or 271D(2) of the Act to the effect that a child witness notice should be lodged or that an order varying or revoking an earlier order authorising the use of special measures should be made. Provisions relating to disposing of child witness notices and vulnerable witnesses applications at the new mandatory preliminary hearings in High Court cases and dealing with applications to prohibit self-representation in cases in which there are vulnerable witnesses under s 288F were introduced in a new version of s 72 of the Criminal Procedure (Scotland) Act 1995 as inserted by the Criminal Procedure (Amendment) (Scotland) Act 2004, s 1(3).

VICTIM STATEMENTS (2004 ACT, S 3)

3 Evidence of vulnerable witnesses at proofs in relation to victim statements

After section 15 of the Criminal Justice (Scotland) Act 2003 (asp 7) there is inserted—

"15A Application of sections 271 to 271M of the 1995 Act in proofs ordered in relation to victim statements

(1) Sections 271 to 271M of the 1995 Act (which make provision as to the use of special measures for taking

the evidence of vulnerable witnesses) apply in relation to a person who is giving or is to give evidence at or for the purposes of any proof ordered in relation to—

    (a) a victim statement made by virtue of subsection (2) (or by virtue of that subsection and subsection (6)) of section 14 of this Act, or

    (b) a statement made by virtue of subsection (3) of that section in relation to such a victim statement,

as they apply to a person who is giving or is to give evidence at, or for the purposes of, a trial.

(2) For that purpose, any reference in those sections to the trial or trial diet is to be read as a reference to the proof.

(3) Where—

    (a) any person who is giving or is to give evidence at any proof ordered in relation to any such statement as is mentioned in subsection (1) above gave evidence at or for the purposes of any trial in respect of the offence to which the statement relates, and

    (b) a special measure or combination of special measures was used by virtue of sections 271A, 271C or 271D of the 1995 Act for the purpose of taking the person's evidence at the trial,

that special measure or, as the case may be, combination of special measures is to be treated as having been authorised, by virtue of the same section of the 1995 Act, to be used for the purpose of taking the person's evidence at or for the purposes of the proof.

(4) Subsection (3) above does not affect the operation, by virtue of subsection (1) above, of section 271D of the 1995 Act.".

Section 3 of the 2004 Act inserts s 15A into the Criminal Justice (Scotland) Act 2003. Section 15A provides that ss 271–271M apply in relation to a child or adult vulnerable witness who is giving or is to give evidence at or for the purposes of any proof ordered in relation to a victim statement or a supplementary victim statement. Where the matter has already proceeded to trial, the same special measure or measures that were authorised to be used for the purposes of the trial are treated as having been authorised for the purposes of the proof. The measures are subject to review on the motion of the citing party or the court under s 271D. The provisions on victim statements are contained in ss 14 and 15 of the Criminal Justice (Scotland) Act 2003. A 2-year pilot study of victim statement schemes operated at the courts at Ayr, Edinburgh and Kilmarnock between 2003 and 2005. The findings of research into the operation of the schemes were published in March 2007. At present s 15A is not in force. However, on 27 April 2008; Scottish Justice Minister Kenny MacAskill announced the introduction of a national victim statement scheme in solemn cases only, with effect from 1 April 2009.

PRE-TRIAL IDENTIFICATION EVIDENCE (2004 ACT, S 4)

4 Evidence of identification prior to trial

After section 281 of the 1995 Act there is inserted—

"281A Routine evidence: reports of identification prior to trial

(1) Where in a trial the prosecutor lodges as a production a report naming—
  (a) a person identified in an identification parade or other identification procedure by a witness, and
  (b) that witness,
  it shall be presumed, subject to subsection (2) below, that the person named in the report as having been identified by the witness is the person of the same name who appears in answer to the indictment or complaint.

(2) That presumption shall not apply—
  (a) unless the prosecutor has, not less than 14 clear days before the trial, served on the accused a copy of the report and a notice that he intends to rely on the presumption, or
  (b) if the accused—
    (i) not more than 7 days after the date of service of the copy of the report, or
    (ii) by such later time as the court may in special circumstances allow,
  has served notice on the prosecutor that he intends to challenge the facts stated in the report.".

Section 4 of the 2004 Act inserts a new s 281A into the 1995 Act. It extends the provisions on "routine evidence" to reports of proceedings at identification parades. It provides that where, in a trial, the prosecutor lodges as a production a report in which a person identified in an identification parade or other identification procedure by a witness and that witness are named, it will be presumed that the person named in the report as having been identified by the witness is the person who appears in answer to the indictment or the complaint. For the presumption to apply, not less than 14 clear days before the preliminary hearing in High Court cases or the trial in any other case, the prosecutor must serve a copy of the report on the accused along with a notice that he intends to rely on the presumption. If, not more than 7 days after the service of the copy of the report, the accused serves a notice on the prosecutor that he intends to challenge the facts stated in the report, the presumption does not apply. A notice of intention to rely on the presumption should be in Form 21.6-A (r 21.6(1)). Notices of intention to challenge the facts in the report should be in Form 21.6-B (r 21.6(2)).

Section 281A applies to all witnesses and not just those classed as vulnerable. It should reduce the risk of cases in which special measures are used failing for want of corroborated evidence of the identity of the accused as the alleged perpetrator of the charges specified in the complaint or the indictment. In *P* v *Williams* 2005 SLT 508, the accused's former partner identified him in court as the perpetrator of an assault. Child witnesses who used a screen to give their evidence testified that the perpetrator of the assault was known to them as "Dad" or "Big B", but they did not make a visual identification of the accused in court. If such a case were to arise now, provided that the witness had made a visual identification at an identification parade, and the prosecutor had adopted the procedure set out in s 281A, the witness need not make a dock identification.

EXPERT EVIDENCE AS TO SUBSEQUENT BEHAVIOUR (1995 ACT, S 275C)

After s 275B of the 1995 Act there is inserted:

275C Expert evidence as to subsequent behaviour of complainer in certain cases

(1) This section applies in the case of proceedings in respect of any offence to which section 288C of this Act applies.

(2) Expert psychological or psychiatric evidence relating to any subsequent behaviour or statement of the complainer is admissible for the purpose of rebutting any inference adverse to the complainer's credibility or reliability as a witness which might otherwise be drawn from the behaviour or statement.

(3) In subsection (2) above—

"complainer" means the person against whom the offence to which the proceedings relate is alleged to have been committed,

"subsequent behaviour or statement" means any behaviour or statement subsequent to, and not forming part of the acts constituting, the offence to which the proceedings relate and which is not otherwise relevant to any fact in issue at the trial.

(4) This section does not affect the admissibility of any evidence which is admissible otherwise than by virtue of this section.

This section is intended to address the difficulty sometimes faced by complainers in historic sexual abuse cases who may only have disclosed the conduct complained of a lengthy period after it allegedly took place. Such witnesses can find themselves compelled, usually in the course of cross-examination, to explain their reasons for this. There is a risk that the explanation given may raise questions as to the credibility or reliability of the witness even though the trier or triers of fact may have no contextual evidence to assist them in deciding whether such behaviour is reasonable or commonly encountered.

Prior to the introduction of s 5 of the 2004 Act which inserted a new s 275C into the 1995 Act, expert psychological or psychiatric evidence was usually admissible only if it related to behaviour that constituted mental illness or some other abnormality (*Galbraith* v *HM Advocate* 2002 JC 1). Evidence, other than the evidence of the witness him- or herself, which had a bearing on that witness's credibility, was thought to be inadmissible unless the facts were also relevant to the questions at issue in the case (*R* v *Turner* [1975] 1 QB 834, followed in *HM Advocate* v *Grimmond* 2002 SLT 508).

Section 275C can be used by the Crown only and applies to complainers in proceedings for any offence to which s 288C of the 1995 Act applies. These are the common law and statutory sexual offences or any other offence where the court is satisfied that there is a substantial sexual element in the commission of the alleged offence. The witness need not be vulnerable in terms of s 271(1)(a) or (b). Expert psychological or psychiatric evidence relating to any subsequent behaviour or statement of the complainer is admissible for the restricted purpose of rebutting any inference adverse to the complainer's credibility or reliability as a witness which might otherwise be drawn from the behaviour or statement. The provision was introduced into the Vulnerable Witnesses (Scotland) Bill following the refusal of the court in *HM Advocate* v *Grimmond* to admit such evidence. Prior to this enactment, such evidence was not admissible and any assessment of the witness's credibility and reliability was solely a matter for the court or the jury.

Section 275C is intended to address the situation in which a complainer's credibility or reliability is subject to challenge because he or she appears to have acted in an unusual, but not necessarily an abnormal, way. For example, a complainer might only have revealed that he or she had been the victim of sexual abuse many years after the event or, as in *HM Advocate* v *Grimmond,* have disclosed the alleged abuse in stages. In such cases evidence from an appropriately qualified and experienced witness might assist finders of fact to place the evidence they hear in context. Otherwise they could be faced with a choice between a witness's reasons for non-disclosure and the defence's suggestion that an adverse inference could be drawn from such an activity, without having any background information upon which to base their decision other than their own beliefs and prejudices about what they would expect the witness to do in such circumstances. However, expert witnesses will be required to take care not to give their own opinion as to the witness's credibility and so usurp the function of the jury. Their role will be limited to enabling the jury to understand a possible reason for the witness's behaviour, but it will still be a matter for the jury to accept or reject that explanation.

The section has been criticised for applying to sexual offences only (see L Gillespie, "Expert Evidence and Credibility", 2005 SLT (Notes) 53–59) and this does seem unnecessarily prescriptive. In cases of domestic violence or historic non-sexual abuse it is still not possible to lead evidence in order to rebut a negative inference which could be drawn as to a complainer's credibility or reliability. There is no obvious significant difference between sexual and non-sexual cases, other than perhaps the element of embarrassment of testifying in relation to intimate matters.

Section 275C will require the Crown to consider at an early stage in its preparations whether such expert evidence might be required at any subsequent trial and to ensure that its witness is suitably qualified and experienced to give admissible evidence. Any report by the witness would also require to be disclosed to the defence as a matter of course. Provided that the expert is limited to giving evidence which serves to place other evidence of fact in context and has the aim of assisting jurors to reach their own assessment of the credibility and reliability of the witness then s 275C should not prove to be problematic.

Section 275C cannot be used by the accused. However, a number of cases since *Grimmond* have suggested that the defence would be permitted, and in some cases ought, to lead expert psychological evidence which might cast doubt on the credibility of the complainers. In *AJE* v *HM Advocate* 2002 JC 215 and *McBrearty* v *HM Advocate* 2004 JC 12, the court proceeded on the assumption, without hearing arguments, that psychological evidence could have been heard at the trial. Therefore it may be that the limited scope of s 275C will not have an adverse effect on accused persons. Section 275C does not prevent the use of any other expert evidence that is admissible under current law.

PERSONAL CONDUCT OF DEFENCE IN VULNERABLE WITNESS CASES (1995 ACT, SS 288E AND 288F; 2004 ACT, S 6)

Section 6 of the 2004 Act inserted new ss 288E and 288F into the 1995 Act.

6 Prohibition of personal conduct of defence in cases involving vulnerable witnesses

> After section 288D of the 1995 Act there is inserted—
> "Trials involving vulnerable witnesses

288E Prohibition of personal conduct of defence in certain cases involving child witnesses under the age of 12

(1) In proceedings to which this section applies, the accused is prohibited from conducting his defence in person at the trial and in any victim statement proof relating to any offence to which the trial relates.

(2) This section applies to any proceedings (other than proceedings in the district court)—

    (a) in respect of any offence specified in subsection (3) below, and

    (b) in which a child witness who is under the age of 12 on the date of commencement of the proceedings is to give evidence at or for the purposes of the trial.

(3) The offences referred to in subsection (2)(a) above are—

    (a) murder,

    (b) culpable homicide,

    (c) any offence which—

        (i) involves an assault on, or injury or threat of injury to, any person (including any offence involving neglect or ill-treatment of, or other cruelty to, a child), but

        (ii) is not an offence to which section 288C of this Act applies,

    (d) abduction, and

    (e) plagium.

(4) Section 288D of this Act applies in the case of proceedings to which this section applies as it applies in the case of proceedings in respect of a sexual offence to which section 288C of this Act applies.

(5) In proceedings to which this section applies, the prosecutor shall, at the same time as intimating to the accused under section 271A(13) of this Act a child witness notice in respect of a child witness referred to in subsection (2)(b) above, serve on the accused a notice under subsection (6).

(6) A notice under this subsection shall contain intimation to the accused—

    (a) that if he is tried for the offence, his defence may be conducted only by a lawyer,

    (b) that it is therefore in his interests, if he has not already done so, to get the professional assistance of a solicitor, and

    (c) that if he does not engage a solicitor for the purposes of his defence at the trial, the court will do so.

(7) A failure to comply with subsection (5) or (6) above does not affect the validity or lawfulness of any child witness notice or any other element of the proceedings against the accused.

(8) In subsection (1) above, "victim statement proof" means any proof ordered in relation to—
  (a) a victim statement made by virtue of subsection (2) (or by virtue of that subsection and subsection (6)) of section 14 of the Criminal Justice (Scotland) Act 2003 (asp 7), or
  (b) a statement made by virtue of subsection (3) of that section in relation to such a victim statement.

(9) For the purposes of subsection (2)(b) above, proceedings shall be taken to have commenced when the indictment or, as the case may be, the complaint is served on the accused.

288F Power to prohibit personal conduct of defence in other cases involving vulnerable witnesses

(1) This section applies in the case of proceedings in respect of any offence, other than proceedings—
  (a) in the district court,
  (b) in respect of a sexual offence to which section 288C of this Act applies, or
  (c) to which section 288E of this Act applies,
  where a vulnerable witness is to give evidence at, or for the purposes of, the trial.

(2) If satisfied that it is in the interests of the vulnerable witness to do so, the court may—
  (a) on the application of the prosecutor, or
  (b) of its own motion,
  make an order prohibiting the accused from conducting his defence in person at the trial and in any victim statement proof relating to any offence to which the trial relates.

(3) However, the court shall not make an order under subsection (2) above if it considers that—
  (a) the order would give rise to a significant risk of prejudice to the fairness of the trial or otherwise to the interests of justice, and
  (b) that risk significantly outweighs any risk of prejudice to the interests of the vulnerable witness if the order is not made.

(4) The court may make an order under subsection (2) above after, as well as before, proceedings at the trial have commenced.

(5) Section 288D of this Act applies in the case of proceedings in respect of which an order is made under this section as it applies in the case of proceedings in respect of a sexual offence to which section 288C of this Act applies.

(6) In subsection (2) above, "victim statement proof" means any proof ordered in relation to—

(a) a victim statement made by virtue of subsection (2) (or by virtue of that subsection and subsection (6)) of section 14 of the Criminal Justice (Scotland) Act 2003 (asp 7), or

(b) a statement made by virtue of subsection (3) of that section in relation to such a victim statement.".

Section 288E applies to any proceedings, other than those in the district court, in respect of charges of murder, culpable homicide, any offence involving an assault on or injury or threat of injury to any person including neglect of or cruelty to a child, *plagium* or abduction, in which a child who is under the age of 12 on the date of commencement of proceedings is to give evidence at the trial. Proceedings are held to commence when the indictment or complaint is served. It prohibits the accused from conducting his or her own defence at a preliminary hearing or at the trial or any victim statement proof. It is an addition to the measures introduced in s 288C of the 1995 Act by the Sexual Offences (Procedure and Evidence) (Scotland) Act 2002, s 1, which prevents the accused from representing him- or herself in cases of certain sexual offences. Section 288C does not require there to be a vulnerable witness in the case.

The prosecutor must, at the same time as intimating the child witness notice to the accused, serve a notice on him conform to Form 22.7, unless a notice in Form 8.2-C has already been served on the accused along with the indictment. The notice informs the accused that his defence may be conducted only by a lawyer, that it is in his or her interests to secure the services of lawyer if he or she has not already done so and that if he or she does not, the court will engage a solicitor at the preliminary hearing or first diet.

Section 288F empowers the court to prohibit the accused from conducting his or her own defence at the trial or any victim statement proof in cases, other than those in the district court or to which ss 288C and 288E apply, in which a vulnerable witness is to give evidence at the trial. The court must be satisfied that it is in the interests of the witness to make such an order. Orders under s 288F(2) can be made on the application of the prosecutor or on the court's own motion and may be made before or after proceedings at the trial have commenced. The court must not make an order if it considers that the order would give significant risk to the fairness of the trial or otherwise to the interests of justice and that risk significantly outweighs any risk of prejudice to the interests of the vulnerable witness if the order is not made. In proceedings in the High Court, where an order is made before or at the preliminary hearing, the accused is also prohibited from conducting his or her own defence at the preliminary hearing. Where the prosecutor wishes to make an application under s 288F, he or she must lodge a minute in Form 22.8-A with the court, setting out the reasons justifying the prohibition, and serve a copy on all parties to the proceedings. On receipt of the minute, or if the court decides on its own motion to do so, the court makes an order fixing a diet for a hearing of the application and for service of the minute or order with the date of the hearing to all parties and to the governor of any institution in which the accused is held in custody. Hearings can be held in the absence of the parties and where an order is made, the clerk of court intimates the order to the absent party. Where an order is made under s 288F in the absence of the accused, the prosecutor must immediately serve a notice on the accused in Form 22.8-B. The notice advises that the accused's defence may be conducted only by a lawyer, that it is in his or her interests to engage the services of a lawyer and that if he or she does not, the court will engage a solicitor for that purpose.

ENGAGEMENT OF SOLICITOR (2004 ACT, S 7)

7 Special pre-trial procedures for ascertaining in such cases whether accused has engaged a solicitor

(1) In section 71 (first diet) of the 1995 Act—
    (a) in subsection (A1)—
        (i) after "diet" there is inserted "in proceedings to which subsection (B1) below applies",
        (ii) the words from "where" to "applies" are repealed, and
        (iii) for "he" substitute "the accused",
    (b) after that subsection there is inserted—
    "(B1) This subsection applies to proceedings—
        (a) in which the accused is charged with a sexual offence to which section 288C of this Act applies,
        (b) to which section 288E of this Act applies, or
        (c) in which an order under section 288F(2) of this Act has been made before the trial diet.",
    (c) in subsection (5A), for paragraph (a) there is substituted—
        "(a) the proceedings in which the first diet is being held are proceedings to which subsection (B1) above applies;".

(2) In section 71A (further pre-trial diet in sheriff court solemn proceedings: dismissal or withdrawal of solicitor

*representing accused in case of sexual offence) of the 1995
Act, in subsection (1)(a), for the words "charged with a
sexual offence to which section 288C" there is substituted
"in proceedings to which subsection (B1) of section 71".*

(3) *In section 72A (pre-trial diet in High Court proceedings:
inquiry about legal representation of accused in cases of
sexual offences) of the 1995 Act—*

  (a) *in subsection (1), for the words from the beginning to
  "Act" there is substituted "In proceedings to which this
  section",*

  (b) *after that subsection there is inserted—*

"(1A) This section applies to proceedings in the High Court—

    (a) *in which the accused is charged with a sexual
    offence to which section 288C of this Act applies,*

    (b) *to which section 288E of this Act applies, or*

    (c) *in which an order under section 288F(2) of this Act
    has been made before the trial diet.".*

These amendments update that part of s 71 of the 1995 Act which
relates to the duty of the court to discover whether the accused has
engaged a solicitor for the purpose of defending him or her at the
trial. They extend the duty of the court to do so in cases to which
s 288E applies or in respect of which an order under s 288F has been
made before the trial diet.

PRECOGNITION BY ACCUSED (2004 ACT, S 8)

8 Prohibition of precognition by accused in person of child witnesses under 12 in cases to which section 288E applies

*In section 291 (precognition on oath of defence witnesses)
of the 1995 Act, after subsection (5) there is inserted—*

*"(6) A warrant is not to be granted under this section for
the citation for precognition by the accused in person of
any child under the age of 12 on the relevant date where
the offence in relation to which the child is alleged to
be a witness is one specified in section 288E(3) of this
Act.*

(7) *In subsection (6) above, "the relevant date" means—*

  (a) *where an indictment or complaint in respect of the
  offence has been served on the accused at the time
  of the application, the date on which the indictment
  or complaint was so served, or*

  (b) *where an indictment or complaint in respect of
  the offence has not been so served, the date on
  which the application under subsection (1) above is
  made.".*

The intention of ss 288C, 288E and 288F were to prevent the accused from representing him- or herself and therefore cross-examining the victim of a sexual offence, a child under the age of 12 or other vulnerable witness. This amendment to s 291 of the 1995 Act extends this prohibition to the precognition on oath of such witnesses by the accused in person.

PRE-TRIAL PROCEDURE IN SHERIFF COURT SUMMARY PROCEEDINGS (2004 ACT, S 9)

9 Summary proceedings in sheriff court: pre-trial procedure where no intermediate diet is fixed

After section 148A of the 1995 Act there is inserted—

"148B Pre-trial procedure in sheriff court where no intermediate diet is fixed

(1) Where, in any summary proceedings in the sheriff court, no intermediate diet is fixed, the court shall, at the trial diet before the first witness is sworn—

  (a) ascertain whether subsection (2) below applies to any person who is to give evidence at or for the purposes of the trial or to the accused and, if so, consider whether it should make an order under section 271A(7) or 271D(2) of this Act in relation to the person or, as the case may be, the accused, and

  (b) if—

    (i) section 288E of this Act applies to the proceedings, or

    (ii) an order under section 288F(2) has been made in the proceedings,

  ascertain whether or not the accused has engaged a solicitor for the purposes of his defence at the trial.

(2) This subsection applies—

  (a) to a person who is to give evidence at or for the purposes of the trial if that person is, or is likely to be, a vulnerable witness,

  (b) to the accused if, were he to give evidence at or for the purposes of the trial, he would be, or be likely to be, a vulnerable witness.

(3) Where, following inquiries for the purposes of subsection (1)(b) above, it appears to the court that the accused has not engaged a solicitor for the purposes of his defence at the trial, the court may adjourn the trial diet for a period of not more than 48 hours and ordain the accused then to attend.

(4) At the trial diet, the court may ask the prosecutor and the accused any question in connection with any matter which it is required to ascertain or consider under subsection (1) above.".

This new s 148B takes account of the situation where in summary proceedings a trial has been fixed but no intermediate diet took place in advance of that trial diet. In such cases, before the first witness is sworn, the court must ascertain whether there are any vulnerable witnesses in the case and, if so, consider whether to make an order that a child witness notice be lodged or to revoke or vary an order already made under either s 271A or s 271C. In addition, if the case is one to which s 288E applies or an order under s 288F has been made, the court must find out whether the accused has appointed a solicitor to represent him or her at the trial. If he or she has not, the court may adjourn the diet for not more than 48 hours for him or her to do so. The court is permitted to ask the prosecutor and the accused such questions as it sees fit in order to comply with its duty under s 148B(1).

6 CIVIL PROCEEDINGS AND VULNERABLE WITNESSES: SCOPE AND PROCEDURES

Civil proceedings were the last in line to benefit from implementation of the 2004 Act, on 1 November 2007, but the specific needs of vulnerable witnesses had been under consideration since the publication of *Towards a Just Conclusion* by the Scottish Office in 1998. At the public launch of that publication the Minister Henry McLeish recalled his own anxiety in connection with giving evidence in civil proceedings relating to anti-social tenants in his council ward, and welcomed the discussion about appropriate support for witnesses in civil cases. In fact, within that publication (Chapter 7) a relatively "light touch" approach was advocated, using the differences between the civil and criminal context to draw away from proposing any substantive changes in law to support vulnerable witnesses. The lack of a corroboration requirement and the scope for admission of hearsay in written, recorded or oral form were used to justify recommendations that existing methods could be used to save the witness the distress of appearing in court. The fact that a rule existed for child care proceedings to allow evidence by television link prompted the observation in *Towards a Just Conclusion* that civil courts in other proceedings could opt for a similar process of receiving evidence, although neither statute nor common law expressly allowed for it. It was proposed that those responsible for bringing evidence to court in civil proceedings (the parties and their agents) should be alert to witness needs and think creatively about how the evidence could be led and the witness supported within the existing civil regime.

However, the responses to the 2002 consultation paper *Vital Voices: Helping Vulnerable Witnesses Give Evidence* and the subsequent *Vital Voices* policy statement published in 2003 favoured the adoption of specific statutory reform for civil cases and acknowledged that "children and mentally ill people can be vulnerable as witnesses in *any* court case and other people can be vulnerable due to the nature of their evidence or because they have experienced distress due to previous harassment or discrimination" (Policy Statement, para 3.2).

CIVIL PROVISIONS IN THE 2004 ACT

Sections 11–23 of the 2004 Act deal with civil matters and s 24 (competence of witnesses) applies in both civil and criminal proceedings. Competence is examined fully in Chapter 7. The text of s 11 is given in Chapter 1 (pages 8–10). The civil proceedings to which the Act applies are defined broadly in s 11. They embrace civil proceedings in any of the ordinary courts of law, and any proceedings in court under the Children (Scotland) Act 1995 (which are in themselves termed "civil proceedings"), but in respect of which special rules of procedure may have been made under s 91 of that Act. Those special rules are, at the date of writing, the Act of Sederunt (Child Care and Maintenance) Rules 1997 (SI 1997/291), as amended. Those rules have provided since 1997 for taking a child's evidence by live television link in that limited range of child protection proceedings in court to which the Act of Sederunt applies. Until the enactment of the 2004 Act these were the only statutory provisions envisaging special measures in civil cases.

The remaining civil proceedings to which the 2004 Act applies are described by the mysterious title of "such proceedings in any of the ordinary courts of law". It is no doubt intended that this will mean any civil proceedings other than those *sui generis* proceedings concerning children specifically mentioned above. The use of the word "ordinary" is slightly confusing in that in a civil context it tends to bring to mind the ordinary cause court before the sheriff within which most civil proceedings in Scotland are conducted. However, the intention is clearly to be inclusive and it becomes clearer from the range of Acts of Sederunt promulgated following the 2004 Act that proceedings across the whole civil spectrum are anticipated – from the Court of Session summons and petition procedures to summary causes, small claims, summary applications and other specific civil procedures under statute (for example, proceedings under insolvency legislation). Accordingly the provisions might apply to anything from an action for proving the tenor of a document in the Court of Session, to an application under the Adults with Incapacity (Scotland) Act 2000, to an action for damages for personal injury. However, tribunal proceedings do not fall within the definition and one would have to look to the rules of a particular tribunal to seek authority for special measures. For example, the Mental Health Tribunal for Scotland (Practice and Procedure) Rules 2005 (SSI 2005/420), r 71 allows a tribunal to decide to allow evidence of a witness who is unable to attend personally in any way or form that it thinks fit, including by video link.

11 Interpretation of this Part

(1) For the purposes of this Part of this Act, a person who is giving or is to give evidence in or for the purposes of any civil proceedings is a vulnerable witness if—

   (a) the person is under the age of 16 on the date of commencement of the proceedings (such a vulnerable witness being referred to in this Part as a "child witness"), or

    (b) where the person is not a child witness, there is a significant risk that the quality of the evidence to be given by the person will be diminished by reason of—

        (i) mental disorder (within the meaning of section 328 of the Mental Health (Care and Treatment) (Scotland) Act 2003 (asp 13)), or

        (ii) fear or distress in connection with giving evidence in the proceedings.

(2) In considering whether a person is a vulnerable witness by virtue of subsection (1)(b) above, the court must take into account—

    (a) the nature and circumstances of the alleged matter to which the proceedings relate,

    (b) the nature of the evidence which the person is likely to give,

    (c) the relationship (if any) between the person and any party to the proceedings,

    (d) the person's age and maturity,

    (e) any behaviour towards the person on the part of—

        (i) any party to the proceedings,

        (ii) members of the family or associates of any such party,

        (iii) any other person who is likely to be a party to the proceedings or a witness in the proceedings, and

    (f) such other matters, including—

        (i) the social and cultural background and ethnic origins of the person,

        (ii) the person's sexual orientation,

        (iii) the domestic and employment circumstances of the person,

        (iv) any religious beliefs or political opinions of the person, and

        (v) any physical disability or other physical impairment which the person has,

as appear to the court to be relevant.

(3) For the purposes of subsection (1)(a) above, proceedings are taken to have commenced when the petition, summons, initial writ or other document initiating the proceedings is served, and, where the document is served on more than one person, the proceedings shall be taken to have commenced when the document is served on the first person on whom it is served.

(4) In subsection (1)(b), the reference to the quality of evidence is to its quality in terms of completeness, coherence and accuracy.

(5) In this Part—

        "child witness notice" has the meaning given in section 12(2), *"civil proceedings"* includes, in addition to such proceedings in any of the ordinary courts of law, any proceedings to which section 91 (procedural rules in relation to certain applications etc.) of the Children (Scotland) Act 1995 (c. 36) applies,

"court" is to be construed in accordance with the meaning of *"civil proceedings"*,

"special measure" means any of the special measures set out in, or prescribed under, section 18,

"vulnerable witness application" has the meaning given in section 12(6)(a).

WITNESSES AND MEASURES

12 Orders authorising the use of special measures for vulnerable witnesses

(1) Where a child witness is to give evidence in or for the purposes of any civil proceedings, the court must, before the proof or other hearing at which the child is to give evidence, make an order—

    (a) authorising the use of such special measure or measures as the court considers to be the most appropriate for the purpose of taking the child witness's evidence, or

    (b) that the child witness is to give evidence without the benefit of any special measure.

(2) The party citing or intending to cite a child witness must lodge with the court a notice (referred to in this Part as a "child witness notice")—

    (a) specifying the special measure or measures which the party considers to be the most appropriate for the purpose of taking the child witness's evidence, or

    (b) if the party considers that the child witness should give evidence without the benefit of any special measure, stating that fact,

and the court must have regard to the child witness notice in making an order under subsection (1) above.

(3) If a child witness notice specifies any of the following special measures, namely—

    (a) the use of a live television link in accordance with section 20 where the place from which the child witness is to give evidence by means of the link is another part of the court building in which the court-room is located,

    (b) the use of a screen in accordance with section 21, or

    (c) the use of a supporter in accordance with section 22 in conjunction with either of the special measures referred to in paragraphs (a) and (b) above, that special measure is, for the purposes of subsection (1)(a) above, to be taken to be the most appropriate for the purposes of taking the child witness's evidence.

(4) The court may make an order under subsection (1)(b) above only if satisfied—
   (a) that the child witness has expressed a wish to give evidence without the benefit of any special measure and that it is appropriate for the child witness so to give evidence, or
   (b) that—
      (i) the use of any special measure for the purpose of taking the evidence of the child witness would give rise to a significant risk of prejudice to the fairness of the proceedings or otherwise to the interests of justice, and
      (ii) that risk significantly outweighs any risk of prejudice to the interests of the child witness if the order is made.

(5) Subsection (6) below applies in relation to a person other than a child witness who is to give evidence in or for the purpose of any civil proceedings (referred to in this section as "the witness").

(6) The court may—
   (a) on an application (referred to in this Part as a "vulnerable witness application") made to it by the party citing or intending to cite the witness, and
   (b) if satisfied that the witness is a vulnerable witness,
   make an order authorising the use of such special measure or measures as the court considers most appropriate for the purpose of taking the witness's evidence.

(7) In deciding whether to make an order under subsection (6) above, the court must—
   (a) have regard to—
      (i) the possible effect on the witness if required to give evidence without the benefit of any special measure, and
      (ii) whether it is likely that the witness would be better able to give evidence with the benefit of a special measure, and
   (b) take into account the matters specified in section 11(2)(a) to (f).

Child witnesses

When the witness is a child the 2004 Act requires (s 12(2)) that the party will lodge a child witness notice, and specify the desired special measures or why special measures are not necessary. The statute does not go as far in civil cases as in criminal cases to present the concept of "standard" special measures for children with automatic application failing opt-out. However, the civil provisions (s 12(2) in particular) do assume that a child will give evidence by some special measures unless cause is shown why not, and if the measure applied for is use of a screen, live television link or supporter for the child, the measure is deemed to be appropriate if sought.

Adult witnesses

For adult witnesses a case must be made out that the witness meets the definitions of vulnerability and the test for the special measure sought. The definition of "vulnerable witness" is the same in civil and criminal cases and has been explored in Chapter 1. The party intending to lead the witness must make application in terms of s 12(6) and (7) and in terms of the relevant rules of procedure applying to the civil action in which the application is made.

13 Review of arrangements for vulnerable witnesses

(1) In any civil proceedings in which a person who is giving or is to give evidence (referred to in this section as "the witness") appears to the court to be a vulnerable witness, the court may at any stage in the proceedings (whether before or after the commencement of the proof or other hearing at which the witness is giving or is to give evidence or before or after the witness has begun to give evidence)—
　(a) on the application of the party citing or intending to cite the witness, or
　(b) of its own motion,
review the current arrangements for taking the witness's evidence and make an order under subsection (2) below.

(2) The order which may be made under this subsection is—
　(a) where the current arrangements for taking the witness's evidence include the use of a special measure or combination of special measures authorised by an order under section 12 or under this subsection (referred to as the "earlier order"), an order varying or revoking the earlier order, or
　(b) where the current arrangements for taking the witness's evidence do not include any special measure, an order authorising the use of such special measure or measures as the court considers most appropriate for the purpose of taking the witness's evidence.

(3) An order under subsection (2)(a) above varying an earlier order may—

    (a) add to or substitute for any special measure authorised by the earlier order such other special measure as the court considers most appropriate for the purpose of taking the witness's evidence, or

    (b) where the earlier order authorises the use of a combination of special measures for that purpose, delete any of the special measures so authorised.

(4) The court may make an order under subsection (2)(a) above revoking an earlier order only if satisfied that—

    (a) the witness has expressed a wish to give or, as the case may be, continue to give evidence without the benefit of any special measure and that it is appropriate for the witness so to give evidence, or

    (b) that—

      (i) the use, or continued use, of the special measure for the purpose of taking the witness's evidence would give rise to a significant risk of prejudice to the fairness of the proceedings or otherwise to the interests of justice, and

      (ii) that risk significantly outweighs any risk of prejudice to the interests of the witness if the order is made.

(5) Subsection (7) of section 12 applies to the making of an order under subsection (2)(b) of this section as it applies to the making of an order under subsection (6) of that section but as if the references to the witness were to the witness within the meaning of this section.

(6) In this section, "current arrangements" means the arrangements in place at the time the review under this section is begun.

14 Procedure in connection with orders under sections 12 and 13

(1) In section 5 (power to regulate procedure etc. in the Court of Session by act of sederunt) of the Court of Session Act 1988 (c. 36), after paragraph (d) there is inserted—

    "(da) to regulate the procedure to be followed in proceedings in the Court in connection with the making of orders under sections 12(1) and (6) and 13(2) of the Vulnerable Witnesses (Scotland) Act 2004 (asp 3) ("the 2004 Act");

    (db) to regulate, so far as not regulated by the 2004 Act, the use in any proceedings in the Court of any special measures authorised by virtue of that Act to be used;".

(2) In section 32(1) (power of Court of Session to regulate civil procedure in the sheriff court) of the Sheriff Courts (Scotland) Act 1971 (c. 58), after paragraph (e) there is inserted—

"*(ea) regulating the procedure to be followed in connection with the making of orders under sections 12(1) and (6) and 13(2) of the Vulnerable Witnesses (Scotland) Act 2004 (asp 3) ("the 2004 Act");*

(eb) regulating, so far as not regulated by the 2004 Act, the use of special measures authorised by virtue of that Act to be used;".

15 Vulnerable witnesses: supplementary provision

(1) Subsection (2) below applies where—

    (a) a party is considering for the purposes of a child witness notice or a vulnerable witness application which of the special measures is or are the most appropriate for the purpose of taking the evidence of the person to whom the notice or application relates, or

    (b) the court is making an order under section 12(1) or (6) or 13(2).

(2) The party or, as the case may be, the court must—

    (a) have regard to the best interests of the witness, and

    (b) take account of any views expressed by—

        (i) the witness (having regard, where the witness is a child witness, to the witness's age and maturity), and

        (ii) where the witness is a child witness, the witness's parent.

(3) For the purposes of subsection (2)(b) above, where the witness is a child witness—

    (a) the witness is to be presumed to be of sufficient age and maturity to form a view if aged 12 or older, and

    (b) in the event that any views expressed by the witness are inconsistent with any views expressed by the witness's parent, the views of the witness are to be given greater weight.

(4) In this section—

"parent", in relation to a child witness, means any person having parental responsibilities within the meaning of section 1(3) of the Children (Scotland) Act 1995 (c. 36) in relation to the child witness,

"the witness" means—

    (a) in the case referred to in subsection (1)(a) above, the person to whom the child witness notice or vulnerable witness application relates,

    (b) in the case referred to in subsection (1)(b) above, the person to whom the order would relate.

Applying for special measures

Compared with criminal proceedings where the witnesses for the Crown are cited in the name of the state, in civil proceedings all witnesses are called by a party who may be a private individual or corporation or may be a public body exercising a statutory role in raising or defending the action. The onus lies on the party (which in practice would be via the agent if represented) to make application to the court in respect of the vulnerable witness (s 12(2) and (6)). A party in deciding whether to apply and what special measure to seek, and the court in dealing with the application, must, under s 15, have regard to the best interests of the potential witness, and take account of any views expressed by the witness (having regard to the witness's age and maturity, a child of 12 being presumed to be of such age and maturity as to be able to form a view). Regard should also be had to views of the parent of a child witness (ie a person having parental responsibilities and rights), but in the event of dispute between parent and witness the witness's views should be given greater weight. The factors relevant to deciding whether a witness is vulnerable are also applied to the decision regarding special measures (s 12(7)(b) and s 11(2)(a)–(f)).

Training for prosecutors and defence agents to use the provision in criminal cases was logistically much simpler than trying to ensure that the diverse spread of parties and their agents in civil cases are aware of the opportunities for supporting vulnerable witnesses in civil cases. Training has been organised through national and regional lawyers' organisations. Rules of procedure in child protection cases in court to which the Act of Sederunt (Child Care and Maintenance Rules) 1997 (SI 1997/291), as amended, apply, provide that the sheriff shall ascertain whether there is or is likely to be a vulnerable witness who is to give evidence at or for the purpose of a proof or hearing, as well as dealing with any child witness notice or vulnerable witness application. Rules of procedure for the Court of Session and the sheriff court require the sheriff at a pre-proof hearing to consider whether there is or is likely to be a vulnerable witness and also place obligations on parties (or their agents) to lodge notices or make application and intimate to the opponent.

The issue of fairness of trial for the accused which drives many of the decisions in criminal processes is alien to the civil context, but the proceedings must be fair to both parties in accordance with Art 6 of the ECHR. Fundamental to that fairness is the concept of equality of arms, including the ability to ensure that relevant evidence can be laid before the court, and in a form that presents the evidence in its best light, albeit then subject to cross-examination or comment if such cross-examination is not possible. Special measures, once granted, can be revoked if they put the fairness of the proceedings in jeopardy.

The criteria for determining the vulnerability of the witness and the need for special measures, although expressed in identical terms for civil and criminal cases, may operate to different effect in civil cases. The absence of the jury, the accused in the dock etc may seem to make the civil court less threatening to the witness. On the other hand, the physical proximity of parties to witnesses in a small courtroom used for civil business and the role of parties in instructing agents actively during the proceedings may cause distress to a witness who is fearful of a party or that party's family or associates. In actions arising from behaviour within families (eg divorce, contact, child protection proceedings) there may be much closer relationships between witness and parties than in many criminal cases. A witness or party may even feel intimidated by the amount of money involved and perceived social, cultural or economic weakness compared with a more powerful party whose success may bring financial ruin. Also, in civil cases there is no restriction on the power of a party to conduct the proceedings in person without representation, even if there is a vulnerable witness, which may be another factor making the civil courtroom more intimidating than first thought. Hence the distress to the witness that may be averted in certain criminal cases by ss 288 *et seq* prohibiting the accused from conducting his or her own defence is not manageable in civil cases other than by use of special measures under the 2004 Act and common law powers of the court to regulate the fairness of the proceedings.

16 Party to proceedings as a vulnerable witness

> Where a child witness or other person who is giving or is to give evidence in or for the purposes of any civil proceedings (referred to in this section as "the witness") is a party to the proceedings—
>
> (a) sections 12 and 13 have effect in relation to the witness as if references in those sections to the party citing or intending to cite the witness were references to the witness, and
>
> (b) section 15 has effect in relation to the witness as if—
>
>> (i) in subsection (1), paragraph (a) were omitted, and
>>
>> (ii) in subsection (2), the words "The party or, as the case may be," were omitted.

Vulnerable party

Section 16 extends the potential for special measures to a party who is a child or an adult who meets the vulnerability definition. That party may make the application on his or her own account (s 16(a)) but is not expressly required to take account of his or her own views and interests (or the views of a parent if the party is a child) since s 16(b) disapplies the tests in s 15(1)(a) and (2) from the party applying on his or her own behalf, leaving it only to the court to have regard to these factors in determining the application.

SPECIAL MEASURES AND REVIEW

19 Taking of evidence by a commissioner

(1) Where the special measure to be used is taking of evidence by a commissioner, the court must appoint a commissioner to take the evidence of the vulnerable witness in respect of whom the special measure is to be used.

(2) Proceedings before a commissioner appointed under subsection (1) above must be recorded by video recorder.

(3) A party to the proceedings—
   (a) must not, except by leave of the court, be present in the room where such proceedings are taking place, but
   (b) is entitled by such means as seem suitable to the court to watch and hear the proceedings.

(4) The recording of the proceedings made in pursuance of subsection (2) above is to be received in evidence without being sworn to by witnesses.

20 Live television link

(1) Where the special measure to be used is a live television link, the court must make such arrangements as seem to it appropriate for the vulnerable witness in respect of whom the special measure is to be used to give evidence by means of such a link.

(2) Where—
   (a) the live television link is to be used in proceedings in a sheriff court, but
   (b) that court lacks accommodation or equipment necessary for the purpose of receiving such a link,
   the sheriff may by order transfer the proceedings to any sheriff court in the same sheriffdom which has such accommodation or equipment available.

(3) An order may be made under subsection (2) above—
   (a) at any stage in the proceedings (whether before or after the commencement of the proof or other hearing at which the vulnerable witness is to give evidence), or
   (b) in relation to a part of the proceedings.

21 Screens

(1) Where the special measure to be used is a screen, the screen must be used to conceal the parties to the proceedings from the sight of the vulnerable witness in respect of whom the special measure is to be used.

(2) However, the court must make arrangements to ensure that the parties are able to watch and hear the vulnerable witness giving evidence.

(3) Subsections (2) and (3) of section 20 apply for the purposes of use of a screen under this section as they apply for the purposes of use of a live television link under that section but as if—
  (a) references to the live television link were references to the screen, and
  (b) the reference to receiving such a link were a reference to the use of a screen.

22 Supporters

(1) Where the special measure to be used is a supporter, another person ("the supporter") nominated by or on behalf of the vulnerable witness in respect of whom the special measure is to be used may be present alongside the witness for the purpose of providing support whilst the witness is giving evidence.

(2) Where the person nominated as the supporter is to give evidence in the proceedings, that person may not act as the supporter at any time before giving evidence.

(3) The supporter must not prompt or otherwise seek to influence the vulnerable witness in the course of giving evidence.

The special measures available in civil cases are evidence on commission (s 19); live television link (s 20); screen (s 21); or supporter (s 22), individually or in combination. The Secretary of State may designate other measures but has not yet done so. These measures equate with most of those available in criminal cases which were considered in detail in Chapter 2. The exception is that there is no special provision for prior statements since these are routinely admissible in proof of their contents under the Civil Evidence (Scotland) Act 1988, s 2. Under s 9 of that Act, "documents" admissible as proof of the truth of their contents in civil cases include written records and mechanical or digital recordings, so prior "statements" could take the form of recordings.

The court is obliged to keep the matter of special measures under review (s 13). This may be done on the application of a party or by the court of its own accord. Special arrangements may be revoked only if the witness seeks to have the arrangement revoked and it is appropriate for the court to do so, or the use, or continued use, of the special measure for the purpose of taking the witness's evidence would give rise to a significant risk of prejudice to the fairness of the proceedings or otherwise to the interests of justice, and that risk significantly outweighs any risk of prejudice to the interests of the witness if the order is made.

APPLICATION AND REVIEW PROCEDURES

For civil actions the 2004 Act dictates only to a limited extent the expectations of processing notices and applications for special measures for a vulnerable witness or party in civil proceedings. The application must be dealt with before the proof or hearing in the case (s 12(1)). The level of detail found in the statutory provisions themselves is much lower in civil cases than in criminal ones. This follows the trend in the civil context to have most of the procedure in Acts of Sederunt rather than in primary legislation.

Accordingly, the procedures in terms of form of application, notice and process for dealing with dispute are to be found in a number of Acts of Sederunt applying to different types of civil proceedings but all triggered by the enactment of the 2004 Act. The primary example of this is the Act of Sederunt (Ordinary Cause, Summary Application, Summary Cause and Small Claims Rules) Amendment (Vulnerable Witnesses (Scotland) Act 2004) 2007 (SSI 2007/463) which sacrifices snappiness of title for breadth and self-explanation. For ordinary causes this introduces a new Chapter 45 to the rules to deal with 2004 Act requirements. In summary causes a new Chapter 18A is added to the rules and for small claims a new Chapter 17A is added. The summary application extensions are now embedded in the rules for that extensive procedural domain, including all applications arising from appeal against a decision made under statute. Hence, appeals against refusal of applications under the Licensing (Scotland) Act 2005, the Road Traffic Act 1988 or the Civic Government (Scotland) Act 1982 if evidence might be allowed are governed by the amended summary application procedures. The Act of Sederunt (Rules of the Court of Session Amendment No 9) (Vulnerable Witnesses (Scotland) Act 2004) 2007 (SSI 2007/450) introduces a new Chapter 35A to the Rules of the Court of Session specifically to accommodate the requirements of the 2004 Act in Court of Session actions initiated by summons or petition.

There are other Acts of Sederunt of 2007 to make provision for notice or application under the 2004 Act that have the effect of amending the rules in proceedings which are specific to subject rather than level or value of case. In particular these relate to company insolvency, bankruptcy and proceedings under the Debtors (Scotland) Act 1987 or the Debt Arrangement and Attachment (Scotland) Act 2002. The Act of Sederunt (Child Care and Maintenance Rules 1997) Amendment (Vulnerable Witnesses (Scotland) Act 2004) 2007 (SSI 2007/468) deals with amendments to those special rules promulgated in 1997 for child protection proceedings in court by virtue of the Children (Scotland) Act 1995, s 91.

The Act of Sederunt (Child Care and Maintenance Rules) 1997 (SI 1997/291), as amended, now requires in r 1.5 that, when the court is dealing with an application to it under the particular rules, "the sheriff shall ascertain whether there is likely to be a vulnerable witness who is to give evidence at or for the purposes of any proof or hearing" as well as dealing with any child witness notice or vulnerable witness application that a party has made (to which notice or application the procedures of the new Chapter 45 of the Ordinary Cause Rules apply).

The amending Acts of Sederunt for the mainstream civil actions have put in place procedures, forms of notice or application, periods of intimation and hearings in the event of dispute, all in relation to child and vulnerable witnesses in civil proceedings as provided for by the 2004 Act. They also impose an obligation on the court to find out whether there is a such a witness not yet identified by the party who intends to lead that witness or to rely on his or her evidence, and link that obligation to specified procedural hearings pre-proof that already exist in that civil process. Hence, in non-family cases in the sheriff court this arises in options hearings and in family cases there it will arise in child welfare hearings. At these stages the court is obliged to explore the question of whether there may be a vulnerable witness (or witnesses) in the case. The equivalent obligation arises in pre-evidential hearings in summary applications and at the preliminary or first hearings respectively in small claims and summary causes. The effect of these requirements placed upon the court to enquire about possible vulnerable witnesses is to counteract the disparity of approach or awareness that may exist among parties or their agents in civil proceedings. They also help to ensure that a vulnerable party witness is identified not only by the request of that party or his or her agent, but by routine question or objective observation by the court.

7 ABOLITION OF THE COMPETENCE TEST FOR WITNESSES IN CRIMINAL AND CIVIL PROCEEDINGS

SECTION 24

Section 24 of the 2004 Act abolishes the competence test for witnesses in criminal and civil proceedings. The section applies to all witnesses and not just those who meet the criteria to be described as vulnerable under the Act. It provides that the evidence of any witness is not inadmissible *solely* because the witness does not understand the nature of the duty of a witness to give truthful evidence or the difference between truth and lies (emphasis added). Thus, the court is not permitted to take any steps intended to establish whether the witness understands those matters at any time before the witness gives evidence.

24 Abolition of the competence test for witnesses in criminal and civil proceedings

> (1) The evidence of any person called as a witness (referred to in this section as "the witness") in criminal or civil proceedings is not inadmissible solely because the witness does not understand—
>> (a) the nature of the duty of a witness to give truthful evidence, or
>> (b) the difference between truth and lies.
>
> (2) Accordingly, the court must not, at any time before the witness gives evidence, take any step intended to establish whether the witness understands those matters.

Prior to the implementation of s 24 of the Vulnerable Witnesses (Scotland) Act 2004 on 1 April 2005, the competence test could and did cause severe difficulties for some child witnesses, witnesses who suffered from mental incapacity and witnesses who experienced difficulties in communication. If they failed the test of their competence to testify, undertaken by the judge in court before they were permitted to begin giving evidence, then the court was barred from hearing their evidence at all. Even though prosecutors would take steps to satisfy themselves at precognition or before issuing a witness citation that the witness would be likely to pass the competence test, the final decision on whether to admit the testimony of a young child was taken only once the trial or proof was underway. This was plainly unsatisfactory as the parties to proceedings had to prepare their cases and the witness had to steel themselves for the experience of giving evidence without it being by any means certain that they would be permitted to do so.

In deciding questions of competence, the court was required to ascertain first whether the child understood the concept of truth and that he or she was under a duty to tell the truth and whether he or she was able to give evidence that was comprehensible.

It was more difficult for a child whose language skills were not sufficiently developed to understand the questions put to him or her or to articulate an account of the allegations being made against the accused to pass the competence test. It was the responsibility of the judge to determine the competence of a child witness after undertaking a preliminary examination of the child and taking into consideration other evidence as to intelligence if necessary. In Scotland there was no minimum age fixed by law below which a child was held incompetent to give evidence. The competence of each child was assessed on a case-by-case basis. A child of 3 years was permitted to testify (*Millar* (1870) 1 Coup 430). Children under 12 years of age were not put on oath but instead were admonished to tell the truth. Children aged between 12 and 14 were to be sworn if the judge considered that the witness understood the nature of the oath; and children over 14 took the oath. The duty to perform the two-stage process was reiterated in *Rees* v *Lowe* (1990 SLT 507) where it was stated that the sheriff or judge was required to "examine whether the witness knows the difference between telling the truth and telling lies and further to admonish the witness as to the importance of telling the truth" (per Lord Justice-Clerk Ross at 509). *Rees* v *Lowe* was followed in *Kelly* v *Docherty* (1991 SLT 219) in which it was stated that the procedure to be followed was in two stages and only after the judge had examined the child himself and if necessary heard other evidence and was satisfied that the child did know the difference between truth and lies could he go on to the stage of admonishing the child to tell the truth.

However, the wide extent of judicial discretion in deciding on the competence of children led to an inconsistent approach. In *KP* v *HM Advocate* (1991 SCCR 933), after only brief questioning, the child was permitted to give evidence. A conviction followed and was upheld on appeal. In another case, a girl of 5 years was held not to be a competent witness after an examination which itself lasted an hour. This resulted in the collapse of the trial of her father on charges of lewd and libidinous practices and behaviour against her and her elder sister who had already successfully given evidence (see K Murray, *Live Television Link: An Evaluation of its Use by Child Witnesses in Scottish Criminal Trials* (Scottish Office, 1995), pp 133–139). Mentally ill or learning disabled witnesses were also required to undergo a test comparable to the one faced by children in order to satisfy the court that they understood the difference between truth and falsehood, that they had a duty to tell the truth, and were capable of giving reasoned, comprehensible evidence. As with child witnesses, each case depended on the condition of the particular witness and the decision to admit the evidence of the witness or not was in the hands of the trial judge who could hear evidence on the issue if necessary (*Black* (1887) 1 White 365).

The need to work through the test clearly and thoroughly before admonition was stressed in the civil case of *R* v *Walker* 1999 SCLR 341. Views were also expressed to the effect that it might be more productive to assess the competence of the witness through the receipt of expert evidence than to try to take the witness through a competence test in open court (*M* v *Kennedy* 1993 SCLR 69).

Competence was assessed at the time of the trial or proof, but if an application was made for a prior statement of the witness to be admitted in criminal cases the court had to be satisfied as to the competence of the maker of the statement at the time when it was made (s 259(1)(c)). Indeed, that provision remains, despite the removal of the competence test for witnesses attending to give evidence. Davidson asks (F Davidson, *Evidence* (W Green, 2006) whether that simply means that all children and vulnerable people are now deemed competent at the date of making a statement or whether account must be taken of whether that person would have been a competent witness under the rules applying at the time when the statement was made. Although it is possible to rely on hearsay evidence in criminal proceedings under s 259(2)(e)(ii) if a child witness refuses to accept admonition or is admonished to tell the truth but refuses to speak, it has to be clear that the court gave the child full opportunity to communicate effectively and there was direct refusal in face of that opportunity (*Macdonald* v *HM Advocate* 1999 SCCR 146).

In civil cases statutory provisions were thought also to require assessment of competence at the time of making a statement now to be admitted in evidence. The Civil Evidence (Scotland) Act 1988, s 2(1)(b) allows the admission of hearsay in proof of its contents only if direct oral evidence on the matter by that person would have been admissible at the proof. After a period of uncertainty, the Full Bench decision in *T* v *T* 2000 SLT 1442 concluded that the pre-condition related to the admissibility of the content of the evidence rather than the competence of the maker of the statement. Although that is not strictly in keeping with the words "by that person" in s 2(1)(b), the words do support an interpretation linked to the date of proof rather than the date of the statement being made.

The main drawback of the traditional competence test was that it did not establish whether the witness could give coherent testimony; instead it focused on whether a witness could understand metaphysical concepts such as truth and as there was no consistent method of applying the test in all cases, it resulted in the exclusion of crucial evidence in some cases when it was admitted in others in comparable circumstances. Section 24 is intended to give all witnesses the opportunity to be heard and to enable the court or the jury to hear all the relevant evidence in a case and to assess the credibility and reliability of the witness. However, it is debatable whether the section is worded in such a way as to ensure this. The inclusion of "solely" in subsection (1) would suggest that if there are other reasons for holding the witness's evidence to be inadmissible then the questions of competency can be taken into account at the stage at which admissibility of the evidence is considered. In addition, subsection (2) does not appear to preclude the parties from embarking on a course of questioning to ascertain the witness's level of understanding due to age or mental illness or impairment at any time once his or her testimony is underway. Although s 24 prevents enquiry as to the witness's understanding of the duty to give truthful evidence, it does not in terms remove the need for admonition of the witness to tell the truth. Accordingly, the rules as to admonition and oath or affirmation for older children and adults seem to remain, but now no witnesses (children or adults whatever their mental capacity) can be interrogated in advance of giving evidence about their understanding of what the oath or admonition will mean to him or her. However, it would be strange if the witness could not be reminded of that admonition and interrogated on that understanding while evidence is being given.

The section does not prevent cross-examination which is designed to challenge the witness's credibility and reliability. Presumably it is necessary to allow the court to direct the jury to disregard evidence where there is clear risk of unfairness to the accused should the evidence be admitted. However, it is difficult to imagine circumstances in which the evidence of the witness is so low in value that fairness to the accused cannot be dealt with by the jury assessing credibility and reliability under appropriate direction from the judge and having regard to any expert evidence that may have been admitted that impinges on the reliability of the witness's evidence.

The way in which s 24 is worded may in fact give rise to concern for certain witnesses rather than for the accused or parties. The guarantee that the witness must be admitted creates the expectation that the witness should be called, but this may be only to face extensive challenge in cross-examination and the risk that very low value or no value will be attached to the content of the evidence. Of course, this section sits alongside the extended definitions and range of special measures, so the capacity of the witness to give the best evidence within her or his abilities should be maximised by those other reforms. However, the adversarial system will result in the weight of the evidence being tested and the witness's expectations of being listened to and believed may have to be carefully managed by the person calling the witness. While the 2004 Act requires the court to consider the best interests of the child in making decisions about special measures in criminal and civil proceedings, that responsibility does not expressly flow through the process of examination and cross-examination. If the civil proceedings in which the child is a witness relate to that child under the Children (Scotland) Act 1995 the court would have such a responsibility, but otherwise the matter seems to rest on professional ethics and the court's responsibilities to oversee fair treatment of witnesses generally.

APPENDIX

LIST OF FORMS OF PROCEDURE

CHILD WITNESS NOTICES

Notices under 1995 Act, s 271A(2), and Act of Adjournal (Criminal Procedure Rules) 1996 (SI 1996/513), r 22.1 and Form 22.1, as amended by Act of Adjournal (Criminal Procedure Rules Amendment No 3) (Vulnerable Witnesses (Scotland) Act 2004) 2005 (SSI 2005/188) and Act of Adjournal (Criminal Procedure Rules Amendment No 2) (Vulnerable Witnesses (Scotland) Act 2004) 2007 (SSI 2007/237):

FORM 22.1   **Rule 22.1**

Form of child witness notice under section 271A(2) of the Criminal Procedure (Scotland) Act 1995

UNTO THE RIGHT HONOURABLE THE LORD JUSTICE GENERAL, LORD JUSTICE CLERK AND LORDS COMMISSIONERS OF JUSTICIARY

[*or* UNTO THE HONOURABLE THE SHERIFF OF (*name of sheriffdom*) AT (*place*)]

CHILD WITNESS NOTICE

by

HER MAJESTY'S ADVOCATE [*or* THE PROCURATOR FISCAL, (*place*)]

[*or* [A.B.] (*address*)

[*or* Prisoner in the Prison of (*place*)]]

Prosecution reference. . . . .

Court reference. . . . .

HUMBLY SHEWETH:

1. That [A.B.], *(date of birth)* [, along with *(name(s) of co-accused)*] has been indicted on *(date of indictment)* at the instance of Her Majesty's Advocate with a preliminary hearing [*or* a trial diet] in the High Court of Justiciary sitting at *(place)* on *(date)* [*or* with a first diet on *(date)* and a trial diet on *(date)* in the sheriff court of *(place)*] [*or* has been charged in the above court on a summary complaint at the instance of the procurator fiscal with a trial diet on *(date)* in the sheriff court of *(place)*].

2. That [A.B.] is charged with *(specify charge)*[, which is an offence to which section 288C [*or* section 288E] of the Criminal Procedure (Scotland) Act 1995 applies][*or* and an order has been made under section 288F(2) of the Criminal Procedure (Scotland) Act 1995].

3. That the applicant has cited [*or* intends to cite][C.D.], *(date of birth)* as a witness who is to [*or* [A.B.] may] give evidence at, or for the purposes of, the trial.

4. That [C.D.] [*or* [A.B.]] is a child witness under section 271(1)(a) of the Criminal Procedure (Scotland) Act 1995 [and was under the age of twelve on the date of commencement of proceedings].

5. The following special measure[s] is [*or* are] considered the most appropriate for the purpose of taking the evidence of [C.D.][*or* the applicant]:-

(here specify any special measure(s) sought)

[and that the special measure(s) of *(here specify special measure(s), other than the standard special measure(s) sought)* is [*or* are] not a standard special measure under section 271A(14) of the Act of 1995.

The reason[s] this [*or* these] special measure[s], other than the standard special measure[s], is [*or* are] considered the most appropriate is [*or* are] as follows:-

(here specify reason(s) for the special measure(s), other than the standard special measure(s) sought)].

6. [*or* Authorisation of the use of no special measures is considered the most appropriate for the taking of evidence of [C.D.] [*or* the applicant] for the following reasons:–

(here specify the reasons for no special measures being sought).]

7. That [C.D.] [*or* [A.B.]] and the parent[s] of [*or* person[s] with parental responsibility for] [C.D.] [*or* [A.B.]] under section 271E(4) of the Act of 1995 have expressed the following view[s]:-

(here set out the view(s) expressed, how and when they were obtained).

8. [That other information considered relevant to this application is as follows:-

(*here set out any other information relevant to the child witness notice*).]

9. That the applicant has intimated a copy of the Notice on [A.B.] [*or* the legal representative of [A.B.]][*or* on the Crown Agent] [*or* the Procurator Fiscal].

MAY IT THEREFORE PLEASE YOUR LORDSHIP[S] -

    (a) to authorise the special measure[s] sought; and [*or*

    (b) to authorise the giving of evidence without the benefit of special measures];

    (c) or to do otherwise as to your Lordship[s] shall seem proper;

    (d) to require the clerk of court to intimate the order to (*specify*).

                ACCORDING TO JUSTICE, etc.

                (*Signed*)

                [A.B.]

                [*or* Legal representative of A.B.]

                [*or* Prosecutor]

                (*Address, e-mail address and telephone number of agent*)

VULNERABLE WITNESS APPLICATIONS

Applications under 1995 Act, s 271C, and Act of Adjournal (Criminal Procedure Rules) 1996 (SI 1996/513), r 22.1A and Form 22.1A, as amended by and Act of Adjournal (Criminal Procedure Rules Amendment) (Vulnerable Witnesses (Scotland) Act 2004) 2006 (SSI 2006/76):

FORM 22.1A   **Rule 22.1A**

Form of vulnerable witness application under section 271C(2) of the Criminal Procedure (Scotland) Act 1995

UNTO THE RIGHT HONOURABLE THE LORD JUSTICE GENERAL, LORD JUSTICE CLERK AND LORDS COMMISSIONERS OF JUSTICIARY

[*or* UNTO THE HONOURABLE THE SHERIFF OF (*name of sheriffdom*) AT (*place*)]

VULNERABLE WITNESS APPLICATION

by

HER MAJESTY'S ADVOCATE [*or* THE PROCURATOR FISCAL, (*place*)]

[*or* [A.B.] (*address*)]

[*or* Prisoner in the Prison of (*place*)]]

Prosecution reference. . . . .

Court reference. . . . .

HUMBLY SHEWETH:

1.   That [A.B.], (*date of birth*) [, along with (*name(s) of co-accused*)] has been indicted on (*date of indictment*) at the instance of Her Majesty's Advocate with a preliminary hearing [*or* a trial diet] in the High Court of Justiciary sitting at (*place*) on (*date*) [*or* with a first diet on (*date*) and a trial diet on (*date*) in the sheriff court of (*place*)].

2.   That [A.B.] is charged with (*specify charge*)[, which is an offence to which section 288C [*or* section 288E] of the Criminal Procedure (Scotland) Act 1995 applies][*or* and an order has been made under section 288F(2) of the Criminal Procedure (Scotland) Act 1995].

3.   That the applicant has cited [*or* intends to cite][C.D.], (*date of birth*) as a witness who is to [*or* [A.B.] may] give evidence at, or for the purposes of, the trial.

4.   That [C.D.] [*or* [A.B.]] is likely to be a vulnerable witness under section 271(1)(b) of the Criminal Procedure (Scotland) Act 1995 for the following reasons:–.

(*here specify reasons witness is considered likely to be a vulnerable witness*)

5.   The following special measure[s] is [*or* are] considered the most appropriate for the purpose of taking the evidence of [C.D.][*or* the applicant]:-

(*here specify any special measure(s) sought*)

The reason[s] this [*or* these] special measure[s] is [*or* are] considered the most appropriate is [*or* are] as follows:–

(*here specify reason(s) for the special measure(s), other than the standard special measure(s) sought*)].

6.   That [C.D.] [*or* [A.B.]] has expressed the following view[s]:–

(*here set out the view(s) expressed, how and when they were obtained*).

7.   [That other information considered relevant to this application is as follows:-

(*here set out any other information relevant to the vulnerable witness application*)]

8.   That the applicant has intimated a copy of this Application on [A.B.] [*or* the legal representative of [A.B.]][*or* on the Crown Agent] [*or* the Procurator Fiscal].

MAY IT THEREFORE PLEASE YOUR LORDSHIP[S] -

   (a) to authorise the special measure[s] sought; and

   (b) to do otherwise as to your Lordship[s] shall seem proper;

   (c) to require the clerk of court to intimate the order to (*specify*).

ACCORDING TO JUSTICE, etc.

(*Signed*)

[A.B.]

[*or* Legal representative of A.B.]

[*or* Prosecutor]

(*Address, e-mail address and telephone number of agent*)

REVIEW OF ARRANGEMENTS
FOR VULNERABLE WITNESSES

Review of arrangements under 1995 Act, s 271D, and Act of Adjournal (Criminal Procedure Rules) 1996 (SI 1996/513), r 22.4 and Form 22.4, as amended by Act of Adjournal (Criminal Procedure Rules Amendment No 3) (Vulnerable Witnesses (Scotland) Act 2004) 2005 (SSI 2005/188) and Act of Adjournal (Criminal Procedure Rules Amendment) (Vulnerable Witnesses (Scotland) Act 2004) 2006 (SSI 2006/76):

FORM 22.4   Rule 22.4

Form of application for review of arrangements for taking evidence under section 271D of the Criminal Procedure (Scotland) Act 1995

UNTO THE RIGHT HONOURABLE THE LORD JUSTICE GENERAL, LORD JUSTICE CLERK AND LORDS COMMISSIONERS OF JUSTICIARY

[*or* UNTO THE HONOURABLE SHERIFF OF (*name of sheriffdom*) AT (*place*)]

MINUTE

by

HER MAJESTY'S ADVOCATE [*or* THE PROCURATOR FISCAL, (*place*)]

[*or* [A.B.] (*address*)

[*or* Prisoner in Prison of (*place*)]]

in

HER MAJESTY'S ADVOCATE [*or* THE PROCURATOR FISCAL, (*place*)]

against

[A.B.] (*address*)

[*or* Prisoner in Prison of (*place*)]

Prosecution reference. . . . .

Court reference . . . .

HUMBLY SHEWETH:

1.   That [A.B.][, along with (*names of co-accused*)] has been indicted at the instance of Her Majesty's Advocate.

2.   That the Minuter has cited [*or* intends to cite] [C.D.] as a witness who is to [*or* [A.B.] may] give evidence at, or for the purposes of, the trial. That [C.D.] [*or* [A.B.]] is a vulnerable witness under section 271(1) of the Criminal Procedure (Scotland) Act 1995.

3.   That the current arrangements for taking the evidence of [C.D.] [*or* [A.B.]] are (*here specify current arrangements*).

4.   That the current arrangements should be reviewed as (*here specify reason(s) for review*).

5.   That an order should be made to (*here specify the order sought*).

6.   That [C.D.] [*or* [A.B.]] and the parent[s] of [*or* person[s] with parental responsibility for] [C.D.] [*or* [A.B.]] under section 271E(4) of the Act of 1995 have expressed the following view[s]:-

(*here set out the view(s) expressed, how and when they were obtained*).

7.   That a copy of this Minute has been duly intimated conform to the execution[s] attached to this Minute.

MAY IT THEREFORE PLEASE YOUR LORDSHIP[S] -

- (a) to fix a diet for hearing this application and to order intimation of this application and the diet to all parties;
- (b) thereafter, after hearing all the parties, to make an order (*specify*);
- (c) or to do otherwise as to your Lordship[s] shall seem proper;
- (d) to require the clerk of court to intimate the order to (*specify*).

IN RESPECT WHEREOF

(*Signed*)

[Prosecutor]

[*or* [A.B.]]

[*or* Legal representative of [A.B.]]

(*Name, address, e-mail address, telephone number of agent*)

(*Place and date*).

NOTICE OF PROHIBITION OF
PERSONAL CONDUCT OF DEFENCE

Proceedings to which 1995 Act, s 288E, applies (witness under the age of 12): Act of Adjournal (Criminal Procedure Rules) 1996 (SI 1996/513), r 22.7 and Form 22.7, as amended by Act of Adjournal (Criminal Procedure Rules Amendment No 3) (Vulnerable Witnesses (Scotland) Act 2004) 2005 (SSI 2005/188) and Act of Adjournal (Criminal Procedure Rules Amendment) (Vulnerable Witnesses (Scotland) Act 2004) 2006 (SSI 2006/76):

FORM 22.7   Rule 22.7

Form of notice of prohibition of personal conduct of defence in certain cases involving child witnesses under the age of twelve under section 288E of the Criminal Procedure (Scotland) Act 1995

IMPORTANT NOTICE

HER MAJESTY'S ADVOCATE [*or* THE PROCURATOR FISCAL, (*place*)]

against

[A.B.] (*address*)

[*or* Prisoner in the Prison of (*place*)]

Prosecution reference. . . . .

Court reference. . . . .

To: (*name*), (*date of birth*), (*address*)

You have been charged with at least one serious offence in which a child witness under the age of twelve is to give evidence at or for the purposes of the trial, therefore -

(1) if you are tried for the offence, your defence may be conducted only by a lawyer;

(2) it is in your interests, if you have not already done so, to get the professional assistance of a solicitor;

(3) if you do not engage a solicitor for the purpose of your defence at the preliminary hearing [*or* first diet] or the trial, the court will do so.

(*Signed*)

Prosecutor

(*Name, address, e-mail address, and
telephone number*)
(*Place and date*)

APPLICATION FOR PROHIBITION OF PERSONAL CONDUCT OF OFFENCE

Prohibition of personal conduct of defence in cases to which 1995 Act, ss 288C and 288E, do not already apply, where the court considers it is in the interests of the vulnerable witness to do so: Act of Adjournal (Criminal Procedure Rules) 1996 (SI 1996/513), r 22.8 and Form 22.8-A, as amended by Act of Adjournal (Criminal Procedure Rules Amendment No 3) (Vulnerable Witnesses (Scotland) Act 2004) 2005 (SSI 2005/188) and Act of Adjournal (Criminal Procedure Rules Amendment) (Vulnerable Witnesses (Scotland) Act 2004) 2006 (SSI 2006/76):

FORM 22.8-A   Rule 22.8(1)

Form of minute seeking prohibition of the personal conduct of defence by the accused under section 288F of the Criminal Procedure (Scotland) Act 1995

UNTO THE RIGHT HONOURABLE THE LORD JUSTICE GENERAL, LORD JUSTICE CLERK AND LORDS COMMISSIONERS OF JUSTICIARY

[*or* UNTO THE HONOURABLE THE SHERIFF OF (*name of sheriffdom*) AT (*place*)]

MINUTE

by

HER MAJESTY'S ADVOCATE [*or* THE PROCURATOR FISCAL, (*place*)]

in

HER MAJESTY'S ADVOCATE [*or* THE PROCURATOR FISCAL (*place*)]

against

[A.B.] (*address*)

[*or* Prisoner in the Prison of (*place*)]

Prosecution reference. . . . .

Court reference. . . . .

HUMBLY SHEWETH:

1.   That [A.B] [, along with (*name(s) of co-accused*)] has been indicted at the instance of Her Majesty's Advocate in the High Court of Justiciary [*or* in the sheriff court] at (*place*) and a diet of (*specify*) has been fixed for (*date*).

2.   That [C.D.] is a witness who is to [*or* [A.B.] may] give evidence at, or for the purposes of, the trial. That [C.D.] [*or* [A.B.]] is a vulnerable witness under section 271(1) of the Criminal Procedure (Scotland) Act 1995 as (*here state the reasons the witness is a vulnerable witness*).

3.   That the Minuter applies for an order prohibiting [A.B.] from conducting his [*or* her] defence in person at the trial and in any victim statement proof relating to any offence to which the trial relates for the following reasons:-

(*here state reasons*).

4.   That the offence in the indictment is not one to which sections 288C or 288E of the Criminal Procedure (Scotland) Act 1995 applies.

5.   That a copy of this Minute has been duly intimated conform to the execution[s] attached to this Minute.

MAY IT THEREFORE PLEASE YOUR LORDSHIP[S] -

(a)   to fix a diet for hearing this application and to order intimation of this application and the diet to all the parties;

(b)   thereafter, on being satisfied in terms of section 288F(3) of the Criminal Procedure (Scotland) Act 1995, to make an order prohibiting [A.B.] from conducting his [*or* her] defence in person at the trial and in any victim statement proof;

(c)   or to do otherwise as to your Lordship[s] shall seem proper; to require the clerk of court to intimate the order to (*specify*).

IN RESPECT WHEREOF

(*Signed*)

Prosecutor

(*Name, address, e-mail address, telephone number*)

(*Place and date*)

AUTHENTICATION OF CERTAIN PRIOR STATEMENTS OF WITNESSES

Act of Adjournal (Criminal Procedure Rules) 1996 (SI 1996/513), r 21.4 and Form 21.4, inserted by Act of Adjournal (Criminal Procedure Rules Amendment No 3) (Vulnerable Witnesses (Scotland) Act 2004) 2005 (SSI 2005/188):

FORM 21.4   **Rule 21.4**

Form of certificate of authentication of documents containing a prior statement for the purposes of section 260(4) of the Criminal Procedure (Scotland) Act 1995

I, (*insert name and designation of person authenticating*), HEREBY CERTIFY THAT this document [*or* the attached document], comprising [this and] the following (*insert number*) pages is a full and accurate record of evidence given by (*insert name and designation of person who gave the prior statement and brief details of the nature, place and date of the proceedings during which the statement was made*).

(*Signed*)

(*date*)

NOTICE OF INTENTION TO RELY ON PRESUMPTION AS TO IDENTIFICATION

Act of Adjournal (Criminal Procedure Rules) 1996 (SI 1996/513), r 21.6(1) and Form 21.6-A, inserted by Act of Adjournal (Criminal Procedure Rules Amendment No 3) (Vulnerable Witnesses (Scotland) Act 2004) 2005 (SSI 2005/188):

FORM 21.6-A   **Rule 21.6(1)**

Form of notice of intention to rely on presumption as to identification under section 281A of the Criminal Procedure (Scotland) Act 1995

IN THE HIGH COURT OF JUSTICIARY

[*or* IN THE SHERIFF COURT

AT (*place*)]

NOTICE OF INTENTION TO RELY ON PRESUMPTION AS TO IDENTIFICATION

by

HER MAJESTY'S ADVOCATE [*or* THE PROCURATOR FISCAL, (*place*)]

in the case against

(*insert name(s) of accused*)

Prosecution reference. . . . .

Court reference. . . . .

To: (*name and address of accused*)

TAKE NOTICE:

(1)   That a report stating the fact[s] of an identification of (*insert name of accused identified*) in an identification parade or other identification procedure by a witness, and the name of that witness, has been lodged under section 281A of the Criminal Procedure (Scotland) Act 1995 by the prosecutor as a production in advance of trial.

(2)   That the prosecutor intends to rely on a presumption that the person named in the report as having been identified by the witness is the person of the same name who appears in answer to the indictment [*or* complaint].

(3)   That if you do not challenge [any of] the fact[s] in the report within seven days after the date of service of this notice it shall be presumed under section 281A of the above-mentioned Act that the person named in the report as having been identified by the witness is the person who appears in answer to the indictment [*or* complaint].

> Served on (*date*) by me by (*state method of service*).
>
> (*Signed*)
>
> Prosecutor
>
> (*Name, address, e-mail address and telephone number*)
>
> (*Place and date*)

NOTICE OF INTENTION TO CHALLENGE FACTS STATED IN REPORT OF IDENTIFICATION

Act of Adjournal (Criminal Procedure Rules) 1996 (SI 1996/513), r 21.6(2) and Form 21.6-B, inserted by Act of Adjournal (Criminal Procedure Rules Amendment No 3) (Vulnerable Witnesses (Scotland) Act 2004) 2005 (SSI 2005/188):

FORM 21.6-B   **Rule 21.6(2)**

Form of notice of challenge under section 281A(2) of the Criminal Procedure (Scotland) Act 1995

NOTICE OF INTENTION TO CHALLENGE FACTS STATED IN REPORT OF IDENTIFICATION

by

[A.B.] (*address*)

[*or* Prisoner in the Prison of (*place*)]

in

HER MAJESTY'S ADVOCATE [*or* THE PROCURATOR FISCAL, (*place*)]

against

(*insert name(s) of accused*)

Prosecution reference. . . . .

Court reference. . . . .

NOTICE IS HEREBY GIVEN under section 281A(2) of the Criminal Procedure (Scotland) Act 1995 that [A.B.] intends to challenge the following fact[s] stated in the report of an identification prior to trial lodged by the prosecutor as production number [*insert production number*] served on (*date*):-

(*here state or refer to the fact(s) challenged*)

(*Signed*)

Accused

[*or* Legal representative for accused]

(*Name, address and e-mail address and telephone number of solicitor*).

APPLICATIONS FOR LEAVE FOR ACCUSED TO BE PRESENT AT COMMISSION

Act of Adjournal (Criminal Procedure Rules) 1996 (SI 1996/513), r 22.14 and Form 22.15, inserted by Act of Adjournal (Criminal Procedure Rules Amendment No 6) (Vulnerable Witnesses (Scotland) Act 2004) (Evidence on Commission) 2005 (SSI 2005/574):

FORM 22.15   Paragraph 2(4)

Form of application for leave for accused to be present during a commission under section 271I(3) of the Criminal Procedure (Scotland) Act 1995

Rule 22.15

UNTO THE RIGHT HONOURABLE THE LORD JUSTICE GENERAL, LORD JUSTICE CLERK AND LORDS COMMISSIONERS OF JUSTICIARY

[*or* UNTO THE HONOURABLE THE SHERIFF OF (*name of sheriffdom*) AT (*place*)]

APPLICATION FOR LEAVE TO BE PRESENT AT COMMISSION

under section 271I(3) of the Criminal Procedure (Scotland) Act 1995

by

[A.B.] (*address*)

[*or* Prisoner in the Prison of (*place*)]

Prosecution reference. . . . .

Court reference. . . . .

HUMBLY SHEWETH:

1. That [A.B.], (*date of birth*) [, along with (*name(s) of co-accused*)] has been indicted on (*date of indictment*) at the instance of Her Majesty's Advocate in the High Court of Justiciary [*or* in the sheriff court of (*place*)] and a diet of (*specify*) has been fixed for (*date*).

2. That on (*date*) an order was made to allow the evidence of [C.D.] to be taken on commission as [C.D.] is a vulnerable witness under section 271(1) of the Criminal Procedure (Scotland) Act 1995.

3. That [A.B.] seeks leave of the court to be present in the room during the proceedings before the commissioner.

4. That [A.B.] can show special cause for leave to be granted as follows:–

(*here state reasons that show special cause*).

5. That a copy of this application has been duly intimated conform to the execution[s] attached to this application.

MAY IT THEREFORE, please your Lordship[s]—

(a) to grant leave under section 271I(3) of the Act of 1995 for [A.B.] to be present in the room during the commission proceedings; [or

(b) to fix a diet for hearing this application and to order intimation of the diet to all parties;]

(c) to do otherwise as to your Lordship[s] shall seem proper;

(d) to require the clerk of court to intimate the order to (*specify*).

IN RESPECT WHEREOF

(*Signed*)

[A.B.]

[*or* Legal representative of [A.B.]]

(*Address, e-mail address and telephone number of agent*).

(*Place and date*)

INDEX

mental disorder
definition, 11

ordinary causes, 77

parliamentary progress of Bill,
4–5
personal conduct of defence,
prohibition on
application, 95–96
generally, 51, 56–60
notice, 93–94
pre-trial considerations
generally, 49–51
identification evidence
challenging facts in report,
54, 100
presumption as to, 53–54,
98–99
sheriff court summary cases,
62–63
precognition by accused, 61–62
presumption as to identification,
53–54, 98–99
prior statement
civil cases
evidence in chief, 21
criminal cases
admission of, 81
authentication of documents,
97
authorisation order, 29–31
evidence in chief, 21–22

review of special measures
civil cases, 75–77
criminal cases, 41–43, 91–92

saving provisions, 47
Scottish Court Service Electronic
Service Delivery Unit
(ESDU), 18
Scottish Executive consultation
paper Vital Voices: helping
Vulnerable Witnesses to
Give Evidence (2002–03),
4, 65

Scottish Law Commission
Discussion Paper (Scot Law
Com No 75, 1988), 3–4
Report (Scot Law Com No 125,
1990), 4
Scottish Office consultation paper
Towards a Just Conclusion
(1998–2000), 4, 65
screens
see also special measures
accused, use by, 45
civil cases
child witnesses, 70
generally, 75–76
criminal cases
child witnesses, 28–31
generally, 18–19
standard special measure, as, 24
self-representation by accused,
prohibition on
application, 95–96
generally, 51, 56–60
notice, 93–94
sheriff court
equipment of courthouses
screens, 19
television link, 17–18
summary proceedings
pre-trial issues, 62–63
small claims, 77
solicitor, accused's engagement of,
60–61
special measures
additional, 13
application for
civil cases, 73–74, 77–78
criminal cases, 25–34, 35–40
child witnesses, automatic
entitlement to, 1
civil cases
application for, 73–74
authorisation orders, 68–69
criminal cases
accused, application to, 43–45
adult vulnerable witnesses,
35–40, 88–90
hearing on use of, 31
review, 41–43, 91–92